D0426202

Marking Time

Also by Michael Korda

Michael Korda

Marking
TIME

Collecting Watches—and Thinking about Time

BARNES & NOBLE BOOKS

NEW YORK

With special thanks to Antiquorum and to Phillips, de Pury & Luxembourg
for the use of photographs, and to Philip M. Poniz for his help, suggestions,
and amazing knowlege of the history and physical design of watches.

Copyright © 2004 by Success Research Corporation

This edition published by Barnes & Noble Publishing, Inc.,
a division of Barnes & Noble, Inc.,
122 Fifth Avenue, NY, NY 10011

All rights reserved.
No part of this book may be used or reproduced
in any manner whatsoever without the
written permission of the Publisher.

2004 Barnes & Noble Books

Designed by Pauline Neuwirth, Neuwirth & Associates, Inc.

ISBN 0-7607-3576-X

Library of Congress Cataloging-in-Publication data available upon request.

Printed and bound in the United States of America

04 05 06 07 08 09 M 9 8 7 6 5 4 3 2 1

For Margaret—again and always

Age cannot wither her, nor custom stale

Her infinite variety. Other women cloy

The appetites they feed, but she makes hungry

Where most she satisfies. . .

And for my friend Edward Faber,

without whom this book would never have been written,

and for whom time is an art, a business, and a passion

Time, like an ever-rolling stream,
Bears all its sons away.
—ISAAC WATTS, 1674–1748

~

He was like a man who resolves to regulate his time by a certain
watch, but will not inquire whether the watch is right or not.
—SAMUEL JOHNSON, 1708–1784

Contents

1

The Gift of Time

HUMANKIND'S PASSIONATE obsession with time—connected to the perceived need for a personal device to measure time exactly—is a fairly recent phenomenon in human history. Our primitive ancestors told time by the sun or by the rumbling in their stomach that warned them when it was time to eat. Darkness told them that it was night, and they drew closer around the campfire or went deeper into the cave. The first faint light of dawn told them that a new day had begun. More than this they did not need to know.

Even the growth of civilization and the building of great cities did little to change this relationship with time. Sand glasses, sundials, ingenious water clocks of various designs, and eventually the first mechanical clocks came to mark time in churches, monasteries, and palaces, but the average citizens in the cities, as in the country, relied on the church bells to tell them what time it was, and agreed to meet after matins, or before vespers. Even in the country, the distant sound of church bells told the farmer when it was time to eat his lunch and when it was time to stop work:

> The curfew tolls the knell of parting day,
> The lowing herd winds slowly o'er the lea,
> The ploughman homeward plods his weary way,
> And leaves the world to darkness and to me.

Thomas Gray's words describe a thousand years of rural life—in England as it happens, but not radically different elsewhere in Europe nor even in the Middle East, except that it would have been the muezzin's call for prayer that marked the end of the day.

Mariners, farmers, soldiers, people who lived or journeyed too far from a city or a religious institution to hear the bells marking the various prayers of the day—all were accustomed to judging the time by looking at the sun, and except on days when it was overcast or cloudy they were pretty good at it. Needless to say, great accuracy was neither expected nor readily obtainable. Mariners were most affected, because the lack of accuracy made navigation a perilous and uncertain art, often bringing ships to land hundreds of miles from where their captains supposed themselves to be, with frequently dire or fatal consequences.

The art of clock making proceeded at a fairly slow pace. For a very long time, size as such was of no importance, because the clock would be placed in a specially constructed stone tower or steeple. By the early part of the sixteenth century, however, clocks were being made that the owner could pick up or place on a table, and from here to the first pocket watches was only a smallish step in what we now call "miniaturization."

It should be kept in mind that the table clock or carriage clock and, even more so, the earliest pocket watches initially were fairly bulky objects, at once a rich man's toy and a symbol of power. These early watches often seem curious to us. They are wound with a key, they have odd dials and sometimes only one hand, rather than the two to which we are accustomed, and are more or less spherical, like a small ball.

Unsigned German pocket watch, ca. 1570, in fitted leather box. Note the single hand, and generous size (64 mm diameter). (Photo by Antiquorum)

Still, the man who owned one not only dazzled those around him with his own wealth and displayed an example of the highest technology of the age (rather the way somebody might do today with the very latest in cellular phones or Palm Pilots), but above all made the point that in *his* immediate environ *he* now established what the time was—an attitude that was to survive, as we shall see, until the end of the nineteenth century in America, where time zones were not established until the 1880s.

Once a man owned a clock of his own and a watch, *he* determined who was late—his immediate world, be it a castle or a palace, now ran on *his* time, not on that of the nearest church or monastery whose bells could be heard over the horizon. This change in attitude is perfectly exemplified in a story about Louis XIV, by whose era the pocket watch had been reduced to a more manageable size, though it was still the most extravagant of mechanical luxuries. Having fixed a rendezvous with one of his ministers at ten o'clock in the morning, he was waiting imperiously, pocket watch in hand, when that worthy appeared before him, bowing on the stroke of ten. "Monsieur," the king said with glacial disapproval, glancing at his watch, "you *almost* made me wait."

The Sun King's remark is curiously modern, anticipating the railway clock, the time clock, and indeed the whole notion of lateness as the supreme example of bad manners and bad planning. Before the watch existed in a practical form, all appointments were approximate in nature, and hardly anything started, or could start, "on time." The powerless waited for days or hours for their betters to appear (and in much of the Middle East and Asia still do), and the powerful signaled their approach with trumpets or bells (depending on the culture), so that those who were waiting for them could stand up, tidy themselves, doff their headgear, and prepare to bow as the great man and his entourage appeared. Times were defined either by prayers or by meals—before matins or after matins, before dinner or after dinner, and so on—and it was generally understood that the less powerful you were, the earlier you should arrive and the longer you would be kept waiting. The emperors of China, for example, often kept foreign ambassadors waiting for weeks or months before allowing them to present their credentials, as a gesture of contempt for "foreign devils" from outside the Celestial Kingdom.

The idea of a man carrying his own means of establishing the time, like most mechanical leaps, must have seemed unimaginable until it happened, but it would remain the prerogative of the very rich for several hundred years. By the eighteenth century, however, the pocket watch was beginning to resemble the now-familiar instrument (though some startling innovations in the design of the dial were already appearing), with an hour hand, a minute hand, and—in the more expensive ones—a small subsidiary dial with a seconds hand. It was still a costly, handmade luxury, however, delicate and difficult to manufacture and repair, ownership of which signified wealth and social position, hence the elaborate watch chain or the watch fob, which announced the presence of the watch even when it was placed safely out of sight in a special, suede- or leather-lined pocket of the waistcoat.

The notion that "time is money" was still more than a hundred years in the future, but owning a watch was a statement of the importance the owner attributed to punctuality, scientific and technological progress, and modernity. What is more, among those of a philosophical turn of mind in France, England, and the North American colonies, the watch came to be seen as a metaphor for the universe, adding a further luster to the ownership of one. Deists, who rejected organized religion and the biblical portrayal of God, came to think of the deity as "the Great Builder," or "the Great Watchmaker," who had painstakingly constructed the whole complex mechanism of the universe, with its interlocking planets, stars, and galaxies, and set it all in exact perpetual motion, a kind of self-winding superclock or superwatch. Elements of this belief can still be found in the proliferation of Masonic symbols on the back of the dollar bill. This view of the universe as a complex mechanism, as if it had been made in Geneva, has lost its appeal since Einstein demonstrated that whatever else it may be, the universe is not a kind of giant and infinitely complex clock or watch, but this idea had a great appeal to educated people in the eighteenth century and helped to make watchmaking a respected profession—a respect that the famous Abraham-Louis Breguet, a daring innovator of watch design as well as the most fashionable watchmaker in Paris, and no fool in business matters, milked for all it was worth.

By the beginning of the eighteenth century, Switzerland had already established itself as the center of a flourishing watch industry, with France and Germany close behind, and by the end of the century Breguet, in Paris, had created timepieces of such breathtaking mechanical complexity and audacious design and decoration that most of his work still seems strikingly modern today. The Breguet "look," with its fine engine-turned dials, delicate hands, and clear numbers is unique and unmistakable, and the quality of his workmanship is amazing. Many of these eighteenth-century watches, if

Breguet pocket watch #1235, sold 14th Floréal, of the year 12 (in the Revolutionary calendar) to James Watt, the inventor of the steam engine. Note the perfect simplicity of the Breguet dial.
(Courtesy of Phillips, de Pury & Luxembourg)

Breguet pocket watch, manufactured in 1799, with quarter repetition and a jump-hour hand. Again, superbly complex— yet superbly simple in appearance.
(Courtesy of Phillips, de Pury & Luxembourg)

properly preserved and restored, will keep time as accurately as the most sophisticated watch available in our day, but of course there was still a major factor lacking in timekeeping— an easy and accurate source by which to *set* the watch. Generally, portable sundials were used to set watches by—not a very convenient method.

Today, we can rely on electronic master chronometers or dial the number of the Naval Observatory in Washington, D.C. (202-762-1401) for the exact time to an infinitesimal fraction of a second, but however accurate gentlemen's time-pieces were in the eighteenth century (and some of them were phenomenal), there was no means of setting them to a universally accepted exact time. On naval ships, for example, the correct time was the time on the captain's marine chronometer (British ships carried as many as three)—Who would argue with him?—and that presented no inconvenience so long as the ship was sailing by itself for weeks or months at a time, but the moment British naval ships joined together in a fleet, all the captains were obliged to reset their chromometers to that of the admiral, however far out his time might be from theirs.

At the dawn of the Industrial Age, none of this mattered much. Timekeeping accuracy was a luxury, an interest of cranks and scientifically-minded gentlemen, but not yet a necessity. Sailing ships left harbor not at a fixed time, but with the outgoing tide (and in any case had to wait on the right direction of the wind); stage coaches left from inns "before breakfast" or "after breakfast"; people set out on journeys on foot or on horseback at "first light." There were no meaningful timetables as such, certainly none on which people could rely.

The invention of the railway changed this situation rapidly. One of the first things railways needed was exact control of time. Unless trains left and arrived precisely on schedule, and unless everybody involved had an accurate watch set to the same time, a train would sooner or later run into the one ahead of it at what was, for the time, high speed, with calamitous and often fatal results. This problem took almost half a century to solve, and involved providing a large number of cheap, reliable watches for railway officials and workers.

Almost everybody who worked on the railways—conductors, engineers, and station masters—needed a cheap, accurate watch, and a train could not be expected to leave, vaguely, "at first light," but instead had to depart at, say, *exactly* 5:06 A.M. Inevitably, passengers had to become time conscious in a way that stage coach passengers had not been. If the train was scheduled to depart at 5:06 A.M., they had to get to the station before then. Train schedules would soon be as firmly fixed in Victorian minds as the Holy Writ (readers of Sir Arthur Conan Doyle's Sherlock Holmes stories will remember that *Bradshaw's Railway Guide* was the constant companion of Holmes's adventures) and as immutable.

The Age of the Railway began only a few years after the Battle of Waterloo in 1815, and men who had fought there lived to accept the railway as a normal part of life—the Duke of Wellington himself, who had commanded the victorious Allied armies, became an enthusiastic railway traveler despite being a witness to one of the first fatal accidents in British railway history—yet the two phenomena marked a profound change in the history of time and of timepieces.

Napoleon fought at Waterloo before the birth of the railways, when time was still elastic and the watch an item of luxury—he lost the battle in part by rising late and delaying over breakfast, while waiting for the ground to dry. Within a generation, a knowledge of railway scheduling and time management in order to move troops would become more important for staff officers than cutting a dashing figure and having a good seat on a horse. In 1870, the Prussians defeated Napoleon's nephew, Napoleon III, in large part because the Prussian general staff had learned to shift vast numbers of men, horses, and cannon quickly to where they were needed by the astute use of railways and railway timetables. A staff officer would henceforth need a good, reliable watch as much as a sharp saber—perhaps more, in fact.

From the 1820s on, men in the industrialized nations consulted their watches, hewed to schedule, and expected that others do the same.† Indeed, for most of the rest of the nineteenth century, the picture of the Anglo-European or American male is that of a bearded man in stiff clothes and a waistcoat, gazing intently at his pocket watch while "the lesser breeds" loll about him, indifferent to the time or to the need to be subservient to it. In Latin America, people said "Mañana," took long siestas, and were invariably late; in the Eastern world, people, if asked when something would happen, shrugged their shoulders fatalistically and said, *"Ensh 'Allah,"* (when Allah wills it); in Africa, the whole concept of time was vague, and "soon" from a native might mean next week, next month, or never. Europeans, however, demanded that things happen on time—*their* time, as defined and measured by the ubiquitous pocket watch.

Because this shift in attitude coincided with the beginning of mass-production methods in the watch industry, the watch soon ceased to be the prerogative of the rich and became part of the normal dress of most European and American men, albeit in silver or gunmetal cases instead of ornamented gold. A watch chain spread across the waistcoat became, in fact, almost a universal symbol of manhood and authority, except for the very poor. The traditional picture of a doctor in the nineteenth century is that of a bearded man seated by the bedside, gravely consulting his pocket watch as he feels for the patient's pulse. Sporting events were timed by equally grave, bearded figures in dark suits, consulting their pocket chronographs. On every railway platform, the station master or one of his assistants stood, magnificently uniformed,

† And women too. I have tried to avoid the cumbersome usage of "he/she" throughout the book, but most statements in it can be applied to both genders equally.

gold buttoned, and bearded, staring at a pocket watch before waving the flag that signaled to the driver that it was time to start the train. Ship captains examined their pocket chronometer before changing course or speed; schoolmasters scowled at their watch while waiting to catch tardy students. There was hardly a profession or a trade that did not involve the watch in some way, if only as the symbol of the British, northern European, and American obsession with time and punctuality, an obsession that remains true today, not unnaturally, in Switzerland, where clocks proliferate in every shape, size, and form, and where every adult male seems to find it necessary to check the accuracy of his watch against that of every clock he passes. In Switzerland of the past, it was not cleanliness that was next to godliness—clean as the Swiss were, in their own view, by comparison with their neighbors—but timekeeping accuracy and rigid punctuality.

In the twenty-first century, we live in a world in which the exact time is so easily and universally available that we tend to take it for granted. Digital clocks tell us the exact time in our homes, our cars, our work places; the exact time appears on our computer screens, VCRs, cable boxes, kitchen appliances, and television screens; it is announced at frequent intervals on the radio and flashes on the little alphanumeric screen of our cellular telephones. The exact time, in fact, is so omnipresent that it's a wonder anybody needs to wear a watch at all or is ever late.

As for the watch itself, some eighty-five years after it was moved from the waistcoat pocket to the wrist (at the request of French officers early in World War I, who complained that there was no way they could pull out a pocket watch to know what time it was when they had a pistol in one hand

and a grenade or a pair of wire cutters in the other), it has been reinvented in electronic, digital form. Some of these watches are so accurate that they constantly readjust themselves to a millionth of a second by receiving exact radio signals pulsating from the U.S. government's atomic clock in Fort Collins, Colorado, or from a satellite high above us.

The amount of technology that can now be crammed into a relatively inexpensive mass-produced plastic digital watch—exact time, date, split stopwatch function, computer function, and so on—is awesome. The real miracle, however, is that watchmakers working by hand more than two hundred years ago could build into a watch most of these functions with intricate mechanical devices and at the same time produce works of art, combining in one piece advanced technology and perfect timekeeping with breathtaking jewelry design.

To collect watches, therefore, is to transform oneself into a connoisseur on several different levels, though not every collector will be equally interested in all of them and may not in fact care about some of them at all. Still, ideally, a watch collector should first of all have a general interest in the history of time—that is, in the whole idea of accurately measuring time as a human need and achievement—then an interest in the technology of timekeeping and how it was refined and developed, and finally a personal aesthetic response to watches as objects of art, design, and, in some cases, popular culture.

Having said which, I must admit that collecting watches is a very diverse phenomenon. Some people collect *only* Rolex watches or Mickey Mouse watches or Bulova Accutron electronic watches or American railroad pocket watches of the nineteenth century or military watches or watches that have been owned by or presented to famous people or rare pocket watches or wristwatches with what are called *grandes complications,* which is to say a bewildering variety of mechanical functions, including, but by no means limited to, minute repetition (the watch chimes to indicate the hour, the quarter of an hour, and the minute at the push of a button), perpetual calendar, phases of the moon, and split-second stopwatch.

There is, in fact, no end to the kind of watch that people collect—no matter how esoteric, rare, and expensive or how cheap, tacky, and mass-produced a timepiece may be, somebody, somewhere collects it, his eyes lighting up at the sight of it. People collect watches with mechanical erotic figures that copulate at the push of a button or on the hour (for some reason, these watches are now popular in Japan and in the nineteenth century were much in demand in Turkey and India) or watches with an elaborate enameled dial or case (cloisonné or champlevé). Some people will collect only watches that have never been unpacked or worn, and remain in their original, unopened wrapping, while others only collect watches that have led interesting lives and passed through many hands. There are collectors for whom superb accuracy is the first criterion, but others who don't ever intend to wind the watch up and use it, and so don't care whether it runs or not. In real estate, we are always told, the three most important considerations about a property are "location, location, and location," but there is no such simple principle when it comes to watches. Condition counts a great deal to some collectors, whereas to others—those who collect military watches for example—condition is altogether secondary; indeed, they prefer a nice patina of wear and hard usage as a sign of authentic military service. Some people collect Pulsar electronic watches—those big, clunky wristwatches with little red plastic screens that light up with digital numbers—while others wouldn't have one even as a gift.

Merely owning a lot of watches, whatever they are and however much they may be worth, doesn't necessarily make them a "collection," however. A collection, by definition, needs to be focused on *something*—a type of watch, a brand of watch, a particular style of watch, a period of watchmaking—if it is to have any serious meaning. A drawer full of watches without any common thread of interest is merely a drawer full of watches, not a collection. It is not necessary to collect *expensive* watches, but it *is* necessary that they represent in some way a special interest or taste on the part of the collector, that they demonstrate a theme, however personal and strange it may be. Mere quantity won't do it.

Part of the reason for people's fascination with watches—apart from the facts that almost everybody has one or more to begin with and that time as such matters to most of us—is that for three centuries they have been not only an expression of humanity's most ambitious and central technology, but one of the very few areas in which lavish personal display for men is considered acceptable, even among people who dress conservatively. Victorian men, for example, dressed somberly and wore little jewelry, except for cuff links, but a gold watch with a heavy eighteen-karat gold chain stretched tight across the waistcoat covering an ample stomach was thought appropriate, even dignified, and not by any stretch of the imagination "showy." Even today, wealthy men who wear dark business suits and who would be horrified by any display of flashy personal jewelry feel no shame in wearing a $400,000 Patek Philippe wristwatch. They might not be comfortable wearing a huge solid-gold Rolex "Cosmograph" on their wrist, which rock stars, superstar athletes, and flamboyant pop celebrities favor, but a discreet gold or platinum wristwatch in good taste, on a black crocodile band, attracts no attention and yet, if it's a valuable collector's item, may be worth up to $4.5 million.

Women can—and do—wear valuable or at least highly visible jewelry, but since the eighteenth century, when men who could afford to do so wore jeweled swords, diamond shoe buckles, and decorative gold buttons, male attire has tended, until very recently, to be more and more drab, and in business circles it remains so. You can go only so far with cuff links and tieclips without crossing the line into Bad Taste. Although such items can be elegant and expensive, they are not particularly collectible, nor are they likely to be works of art or worth a small fortune. A watch, however, is another matter: it can be rare, historically important, beautiful in design, and at the same time unfailingly accurate and therefore practical. No watch is "merely" decorative. No matter how expensive or rare it may be, it must above all be *functional,* that is, "tell time," which means that even the most puritanical of souls is spared the need to feel guilt at buying an expensive or unique one: not only is a watch *needed*—perhaps not this one, in platinum from a famous Swiss maker, but a watch of *some* kind—but provided it is in some way special it can also be thought of as a wise and prudent *investment*, rather than as a huge, self-indulgent splurge.

Indeed, one of the reasons why there are so many watches around to collect is that most of the good ones were made not only to last a lifetime, but to last *several* lifetimes. A watch was passed on from father to son to grandson and beyond, and, provided it was cleaned and lubricated regularly by somebody who knew what he was doing, it would go on keeping time accurately from generation to generation. The notion of "planned obsolescence"—Detroit's phrase for making cars so that you'd need a new one every couple of years—has never been of much interest to watchmakers as a group, whose instinct, perhaps because so many of them have been thrifty Swiss, is to build for the ages (with a few exceptions). What's more, even people who are careless about many other things in life tend to take care of their watches—another reason why watches keep on ticking reliably from century to century. Finally, watches have always been used to celebrate certain landmarks in a man's life—men were presented with a watch when they reached twenty-one or when they married or as a reward for many years of service when they retired. Many of these presentation watches were not only treasured, but carefully preserved for years and years and can still be found in the original velvet-lined leather box, as shiny and unscratched as the day they left the maker.

Even today—despite the fact that watchmakers have tried to make fashion a reason for buying a new watch and have in part succeeded in promoting the watch as if it were an aspect of the haute couture business, or at the very least a fashion accessory—because watches don't wear out, it is hard to throw them away, unlike, say, dresses or shoes that have gone out of style. No matter how chic watches may have become, the damned things *last!*

Patek Philippe, perhaps the most illustrious name in watchmaking and a *maison* that stands for an almost unique level of high workmanship and the highest level of handmade Swiss watchmaking complexity, tries to have it both ways by advertising their watches as both fashionable pieces of jewelry and heirlooms at the same time, the message being that you're not just buying a Patek Philippe for yourself, but for your children and grandchildren, to whom you'll pass it on. The trouble with that notion is that the more fashionable a watch is—the more it is, as the French say, *du moment*—the more old-fashioned and out of style it will appear when your grandchildren finally get their hands on it and the less likely they will be to wear or keep it, let alone thank you for having left it to them, unless it happens to pop back into fashion unexpectedly like 1950s watches.

Other things being equal, watches that retain a classic beauty of design and enduring good taste are likely to survive the longest and to keep or increase their value. The ideal watch is timeless as well as a perfect timekeeper—hence, the continuing tradition of the watch as the appropriate way of expressing gratitude for devoted service or marking important anniversaries or rewarding special accomplishments.

"Giving somebody the gold watch" is still used as a phrase to describe retirement, whether forced or voluntary, and an engraved gold watch is still likely to be presented to a retiring executive or long-term employee. A gold watch given on graduation from university, another old-fashioned tradition, still accounts for a substantial chunk of the business in jewelry stores in college towns.

In the past, of course, this custom was far more widespread. Kings presented those who had done them any kind of service with elaborately engraved and enameled watches, often bearing the king's portrait (the Saudi royal family continues to do so, in fact). Presidents of the United States, from George Washington on, have traditionally presented a gold pocket watch to the captain of a foreign vessel who rescues American seamen (I have seen elaborately engraved examples presented by Presidents Buchanan and Lincoln come up for sale). Hitler presented the meteorologist who gave him a good weather forecast for the invasion of the Low Countries and France with a gold watch, engraved on the back with the Führer's signature and the date of the invasion, May 10, 1940. In the old days in Hollywood, the studio moguls often presented successful directors and actors with an engraved watch to mark the beginning or the completion of a major film. Commodore Vanderbilt presented his son with a richly engraved gold Patek Philippe minute-repeater split-second chronograph and matching gold chain, bought from Tiffany, on Cornelius Vanderbilt Jr.'s twenty-first birthday, in 1893—an object that I happen to have in front of me as I write—and a princely gift it must have been, even for the day, though it, too, ended up for sale after many decades in a safe-deposit box in Palm Beach.

All such watches have been or are likely to end up being sold sooner or later, either privately or in auctions, and the sheer quantity of them is daunting—proof enough that the watch has a talismanic significance that nothing else comes even close to equaling. What's more, the watch as an item to collect has many advantages beyond mechanical, historic, and aesthetic interest. For one thing, you can wear it and use it. For another, it doesn't require you to build a whole building to store your collection, unlike, say, vintage cars, and it doesn't involve you with paperwork and security problems, unlike guns.

Watch collectors, as a group, tend to cherish their privacy. That isn't unusual in the art world. Many collectors don't want any kind of publicity and have no desire to share their collection with anybody, but it's truer of watch collectors than most. Indeed, part of the appeal of collecting watches, I have always thought, is that you can acquire quite a serious and important collection without anybody around you knowing or caring. It's not like arriving home from Christie's with a huge sculpture by Alexander Calder on a truck, or with a large painting or a piece of antique furniture or a Ferrari 250 GTO—you don't need to find or build a place for it or explain to your wife or husband how much money you spent for it. Hardly anybody looks at the watch on your wrist or in your pocket, and the only people likely to notice or be interested are other watch collectors, a fairly secretive lot themselves. Watch collecting in general, therefore, requires no explanations or apologies. A drawer will do for storage (preferably one that can be locked, of course), and because very few people, including your nearest and dearest, are likely to notice that you're wearing a new watch or to guess that it cost a small fortune, it's not likely that each new addition to your collection will provoke an objection. Many of the collections that come up for auction on somebody's death seem to have been acquired bit by bit over the years, a watch here, a watch there, until one day the new widow or the heirs are looking around the house with stupefaction and asking each other, "How on *earth* did he ever acquire so many watches, and what in the world are we going to do with them?"

Like coin and stamp collectors, many watch collectors are fueled with a desire to own every variation, however slight, of a given model or style of watch. Also like coin and stamp collectors (the serious ones, at any rate) they aren't eager to show off their collection, in part out of a justified feeling that others would be bored or wouldn't understand or appreciate the many tiny, subtle differences that make one watch so much more valuable than another that looks, to the uninitiated, more or less identical, and in part from a reluctance to confess what the value of their collection is.

This desire to own every variation has been increased by the watch manufacturers, who, having finally worked out that watches are one of the popular collectibles in the growing "vintage" market, took some time ago to *creating* collectible watches in large quantities. Thus, although it might make sense to a certain kind of person to buy a new Patek Philippe Pagoda wristwatch (a design of the 1920s, so named after the shape of its crystal), it is quite another order of decision to buy a set of four Pagodas, in platinum, white gold, yellow gold, and pink gold, with serial numbers in sequence. That the value of this kind of watch has gone up and up and will go on increasing is fairly certain; on the other hand, that the value of four modern replicas deliberately designed and packaged as a collectible set in a glass-topped wooden presentation box will go on increasing is less certain, particularly because part of the set's value is that it remains untouched and unused, in the original packing—no interesting patina, or signs of wear with this kind of collecting!

Of course, this is not a problem confined to collecting watches. The value of cameras as collectible items has skyrocketed in recent years, and, much as with modern watches, the market is split between those who want a Leica IIIc from the late 1930s, with all the patina and wear that show it was used and cared for by loving hands, and those who want to collect cameras only in their mint state, still encased in their original, unopened plastic wrappings and boxes.

I am of the opinion that signs of age and use as well as a reasonable degree of patina and wear are *desirable* factors, provided the watch hasn't been abused or damaged, but anybody approaching the idea of collecting watches is going to have to decide for himself (or herself) which state is preferable. As in everything else, a collection should be built around the idea of giving its owner pleasure, not pleasing other collectors or satisfying somebody else's idea of what constitutes quality. If nothing else, buy what pleases and interests *you*, and you will have made the first and perhaps the most important step toward assembling an interesting and valuable collection.

A WORD seems in order right here about my qualifications to write this book. I have collected watches for many years. Before collecting watches, I collected firearms, an area in which many of the same questions pertain, such as patina and wear vs. brand-new condition.

Most of the male members of my family were collectors, sometimes on a grand scale, though none of them collected watches, as it happens. My uncle, Sir Alexander Korda, a founder of the British motion picture industry, as well as a distinguished director and producer, collected impressionist paintings once he was wealthy, most of them bought for him by my father Vincent, an Oscar-winning motion picture art director, painter, and noted art connoisseur. Alex loved to be surrounded by beautiful and expensive things but did not have the patience or the interest of the real collector. My father, on the contrary, lived and worked, it sometimes seemed, only to attend auctions and sales rooms and to buy things that caught his eye—paintings, sculpture, furniture, bric-a-brac, prints, books—almost anything, in fact, *except* watches. The third Korda brother, Zoltan (Oscar-winning director of *The Four Feathers, Jungle Book*, and *Sahara*, among others), collected gold coins and knew everything there was to know about that ancient and complex subject. Indeed, whenever he came to New York, he stayed at a hotel on West Fifty-seventh Street, only because Stack's, the world-famous coin shop, was next door, and he could pop in there as he went in and out or have them bring rare coins up to his suite for examination. Like most "gold bugs" of all kinds, he believed that gold was the best investment—a belief easily explained by the fact that he had lived through the hyperinflation of post-World War I Budapest and Berlin, in which it took a whole shopping bag full of paper money—millions or billions of förints or Deutschmarks—to buy a loaf of bread. Tomorrow it might take a wheelbarrow full of paper money to buy the same size loaf of bread, and the day after, who knew? In Hungary, paper money, constantly reissued with more and more zeros, became so worthless that it was printed only on one side, leaving the other side blank. My father had no interest in Zoli's gold coins but believed the same thing was true of buying good paintings, and they were both right. Almost any collectible item of real quality is likely to prove a sounder investment in the long run than an engraved piece of paper, whatever happens to the economy, and watches are no exception.

None of the three Korda brothers, as it happened, ever carried a watch. Alex had a drawer full of them, given to him by all sorts of people, but he never wore one and preferred to ask his chauffeur, his assistant, or his secretary what the time was when he needed to know. My father didn't believe in wearing a watch, and on the rare occasions when he put one on, it always stopped immediately, confirming his view that they were useless. I never saw my uncle Zoltan wear a watch either, though that may be because he believed they were a mark of bourgeois respectability, which he despised. On the other hand, my maternal grandfather, Octavius Musgrove, always carried a gold pocket watch, with a gold chain across his waistcoat, in the manner of an English Edwardian gentleman, which he was, and in the only photograph of my paternal grandfather, Edward Kellner, taken when he was the farm manager for the wealthy Salgo family on the Hungarian *puszta*, a watch chain is clearly visible on *his* waistcoat, too, though whether it is gold or silver is hard to say.

My grandfather Octavius lovingly polished and looked after his gold pocket watch, hung it up every night from a special stand on his night table after winding it carefully when he went to bed, and took it to be cleaned and lubricated every two years by an elderly Swiss watch repairman at a little jeweler's shop in the Burlington Arcade. I know only because I once accompanied my grandfather on one of these Saturday morning expeditions, which always ended with lunch at Rule's, near Covent Garden, or at Manzi's, a fish restaurant in Soho, near Leicester Square.

Neither grandfather's watch ended up in my hands, which seems a great pity—but perhaps not, on the other hand, because they would have reached me before I was old enough to appreciate them. Perhaps the most affecting page in Winston Churchill's account of his own childhood and youth tells how he lost the valuable pocket watch his father, Lord Randolph Churchill, had given him, and then had to admit to it in a letter to that remote and notoriously short-tempered parent. There is a lesson to be learned from this—never give a child anything valuable, which was borne out to me when Alex presented me with one of the watches from the drawer in his desk before I went to boarding school in Switzerland. It was a pink gold Universal Geneve Tri-Compax, a wristwatch of many complications and significant value (inscribed on the back, "To Alex, from his old friend Darryl Zanuck, Beverly Hills, 1940"), which was like an albatross around my neck throughout my school years, because I lived in fear of losing or damaging it. I don't suppose, to be fair, that Alex would have cared—or even remembered that he had given it to me—but *I* cared, and so did my father, who always asked after it whenever he saw me.

It was perhaps this gift, added to the fact that my school was in Switzerland, that started my interest in watches in the first place. Watches were then (in 1947) still Switzerland's major industry (chocolate was the runner-up), and it would be decades before the invention of the quartz watch and then the electronic digital watch provided the Swiss with a broad and unwelcome list of countries that could produce watches much more cheaply and on a larger scale. In those days, the first thing you looked for in a watch was the words "Made in Switzerland" engraved on the back or painted on the dial. As schoolboys, we were taken on field trips to visit some of the major watchmakers in and around Geneva—I remember being taken to the Rolex factory and given my first glance at precision high technology: long rows of men in white lab coats, wearing magnifying spectacles and hunched over brightly lit work tables, finishing and assembling with extraordinary delicacy and in hushed silence the tiny components of a watch. There were other thrills, too: a complicated, pressurized water chamber—like something Captain Nemo might have had aboard the *Nautilus* in Jules Verne's *Twenty-Thousand Leagues under the Sea*—in which completed Rolex watches were tested to make sure they were waterproof; an electronic stethoscope by means of which an inspector could check the regularity of the watch's movement like a cardiologist listening to the patient's heart beat; and numerous photographs of Rolex watches taped to the bottoms of ships or the hulls of submarines for long periods of time to prove how perfectly sealed their mechanism was.

It was quickly apparent to me that a Rolex would be far more suitable for a schoolboy's life than my uncle Alex's Tri-Compax, and eventually, after buying a Tissot, then a Movado, I saved up enough money, what between birthday presents and our very generous allowance, to trade up to a stainless-steel Rolex Oyster and put the Tri-Compax away for safe-keeping. Buying watches was something of a hobby with the boys at my school, and in those days no Swiss village, however small, lacked a brightly lit watch shop on the main street, with displays of what were then, and to some degree still are, the major brands: Patek Philippe, Vacheron & Constantin, Rolex, Jaeger-LeCoultre, Longines, International Watch Company, Omega, and so on.

My instinct about Rolex was correct—the watch was virtually indestructible, even when I wore it skiing, swimming, playing soccer and hockey, and crewing on Lake Geneva. By the time I graduated from school and joined the Royal Air Force at the age of seventeen, I owned a Rolex Oyster watch, which I still wear today and which still keeps perfect time (and has a radium dial that, however unhealthy, can still be read easily in the dark). The watch was with me through my service in the Royal Air Force, and in the Hungarian Revolution of 1956, and I have worn it sailing, SCUBA diving, riding, parachuting, and swimming. It has never missed a beat, and there seems no particular reason why it should not outlast me. Beyond a few scratches on the band, it shows no signs of wear at all after more than five decades of use.

Of course, four years in Switzerland gave me an interest in the Swiss watch business, which was then at its zenith, so I soon learned that the reality of the Swiss watch industry was not quite the same as its glittering facade in the elegant watch shops near the great hotels in Geneva, Zurich, or Gstaad. The watch business, until the mid-nineteenth century, consisted of small entrepreneurs, and most of the parts they used were made by piecework in small villages in the Alps or the Jura, where whole families gathered around the table making tiny wheels or cogs for very little money—an Alpine version of what were called "sweatshops" in the United States. Watches were not made the way Henry Ford made cars at the famous Dearborn plant, where raw steel came in at one end and a complete car emerged at the other. The Swiss watch manufacturers bought in most of the parts, and even completely assembled components, then employed skilled (and nonunionized) labor to put them together and finish each watch itself. Some manufacturers even bought complete movements and placed them in their own cases. For many years, the actual movement of the highly prized Rolex Daytona chronometer was in fact purchased from Zenith and placed inside the distinctive Rolex case, which meant that you could buy exactly the same watch from Zenith at a fraction of the price of a Rolex, but of course without the cachet, or the legend that Steven McQueen and Paul Newman had worn one at LeMans.

Unfortunately for the Swiss watch industry, the general attitude toward watches was summed up in the immortal lines of Graham Greene, spoken by Orson Welles as the charming villain in *The Third Man* (a motion picture produced by my uncle Alex and art directed by my father): "In Italy for thirty years under the Borgias they had warfare, terror, murder, bloodshed—but they produced Michelangelo, Leonardo da Vinci and the Renaissance. In Switzerland they had brotherly love, five hundred years of democracy and peace, and what did that produce? The cuckoo clock!"

Be that as it may, with the exception of Patek Philippe, perhaps the most expensive and technologically advanced of Swiss firms, the majority of Swiss watch companies operated in pretty much the same way in the twentieth century, relying on bought-in parts and, especially for more complicated watches, on bought-in movements. To some degree, of course, this doesn't matter—How many watch owners are likely to take their prized wristwatches apart and carefully examine the movement?—but the increasing interest in watches as collectibles has focused more attention on the issue of the cozy collaboration between Swiss manufacturers who ostensibly are competitors, and has made serious collectors more aware that what's inside the watch is as important, or more important, than what's on the outside. If you're going to collect watches at all seriously, you should learn to pay attention to this distinction.

In any case, by the time I came to the United States for good, in 1957, I knew much more about watches than I needed to know and retained a certain window shopping fascination with them. I spent a great deal of time walking up and down Madison Avenue and Fifth Avenue on Saturday mornings looking at the new models, without actually buying one—as a junior editor and a new parent, I didn't have the money, and, anyway, my old Rolex kept on ticking faithfully.

All the same, I was interested to see what the Swiss were up to, as they suddenly faced competition from cheaper digital watches on a mass scale, and I soon recognized that after a brief attempt to compete with the Japanese, they opted instead for going back to their nineteenth-century roots, once again turning the watch—the old-fashioned mechanical watch, without batteries or digital displays—into an object of luxury, style, fashion, and frank snob appeal. Rather than going down market, they wisely hurtled, after a period of confusion and crisis, up market as fast as they could go, burnishing the reputations of old names and trademarks, raising their prices sky high, and making the watch, as it had been in the nineteenth century, not only a miracle of handmade precision, but the mark of good taste, authority, and social position—something that could not be achieved by a plastic digital watch that you could buy at your local drugstore or supermarket. Yes, the digital watch could keep perfect time and, if you could figure out what the tiny buttons were for, perform all sorts of complex functions, but it did not add a bit to your prestige, sense of well being, or status. The aim of Swiss watch manufacturers became, on the contrary, *status* above all, and even the executives of the Japanese companies that manufactured millions of cheap digital watches aspired to wearing a gold Rolex on their wrist once they had been paid their bonus.

Although the older of the Swiss firms, such as Patek, retained the highest status of all, Rolex, which produced vastly more watches, acquired a status that has less to do with the watch itself than with a certain high-risk, sporting masculinity that surrounds it. To own a Patek is to be at one with oil sheikhs, international financial figures, glamorous celebrities, and people who only travel on their own airplanes; to own a Rolex is to identify yourself with race car drivers, people who climbed Everest, and sports celebrities of all kinds. To own an Omega is to associate yourself with the astronauts, for the Omega Speedmaster Professional was the first watch worn on the moon and bore on the back of its case an engraved certification of that fact from NASA.

It was as if the Swiss had discovered Walter Mitty and learned how to apply the daydreams of ordinary people to the sale of watches. From the very beginning, this plan worked. Brands that had been almost forgotten outside Switzerland—Ulysse Nardin, for example, or Girard-Perregaux, or Audemars Piguet—were brought back to life again and given international stature, and even older firms that had all but vanished were successfully re-created to take advantage of their name. Nor were the Swiss the only ones to fight back successfully against the tidal wave of cheap digital watches from Asia—the old German watchmaking firms, once in every way equal to the Swiss in quality, famous brand names in Germany, but almost unknown outside it, fought for their share of the international luxury watch market with startling new watches from A. Lange & Söhne, among others.

The difficulty that even a relatively inexpensive watch of good quality is likely to last much longer than its owner was solved first by making the watch a fashion accessory, and then by creating a vast secondary market in which watches that might once have been described as "used" or "secondhand" became "vintage" or "classic" or "collectible" watches, a move made possible by the fact that some large watch stores were willing, very discreetly, to take your current watch, if it was any good, as trade-in on a better one.

Thus, the auctioning and selling of "vintage" watches—some of them not vintage at all, but brand-new—at a fraction of the price the customer would have paid in a watch store went from being a small business to a major one, played out in the limelight. As new watches by firms such as Cartier or Lange or Jaeger-LeCoultre became fashionable, expensive items with an internationally chic reputation, the old watches from the 1920s or the nineteenth century by the same manufacturers leapt in value, too. Watch collecting was no longer something for the specialist, but part of the big-time art business.

Much of this began to take place about the time that I wrote a couple of bestselling novels that were made into miniseries, so that I had, it appeared at the time, money to burn. I also had friends—Morton Janklow, the lawyer/agent, and Robert Bookman, a major player in Hollywood—who collected watches, Janklow favoring Patek Philippe wristwatches and Bookman looking for Cartier wristwatches of the 1920s. I put a modest toe in the water and bought a watch I had always wanted, a Patek Philippe Calatrava from the 1950s, not by accident made at about the time I had been in school in Switzerland. Without giving the matter much thought, I in fact would end up buying just those watches that I had envied on the wrists of my wealthier schoolmates back then. In the vintage automobile business (as opposed to the less-elevated "used car" market) this is known as the "Corvette Syndrome," used to describe a man who has made money by the time he is forty or fifty and is determined to buy the car he always wanted when he was eighteen and it was merely a dream. That explains the number of men in their fifties driving restored thirty-year-old Corvettes or Ferraris and looking as if they needed a giant shoehorn to squeeze themselves into the driver's seat.

In any event, I ended up buying a great many wristwatches that I remembered from my schooldays, and it took a while before it sank in that although there was nothing wrong with doing so, it wasn't a *collection*. It was just a drawer full of pretty nice watches. Nobody except Mort Janklow and Bob Bookman seemed to notice that what I was wearing on my wrist was anything special, and my wife never complained when I bought a new one, because she never looked at my watch.

Pocket watches, perhaps because of my grandfathers, have always fascinated me, and at some point I grew more interested in them and began to read a bit about them. To me, they seemed much more interesting than wristwatches, so eventually I sold all my wristwatches and started to buy pocket watches. Here, too, at first I simply bought what caught my attention for one reason or another and ended up with a drawer full of pocket watches that interested nobody, not even Mort or Bob, and it took a while before I worked out in my own mind that the key to collecting was *specialization*—limiting yourself to an identifiable brand, period, type of watch, rather than being spread out all over the lot.

In the end, I sold everything and started again. I choose to collect only Patek Philippe pocket watches, because Patek was and remains the preeminent name in watchmaking, and to collect only those watches made between 1870 and 1914, the great period for the pocket watch, when the dials were still made of enamel and hand painted. To add a further challenge, I decided to collect only watches that had at least one or two interesting "complications" (minute repetition, split chronograph, perpetual calendar, and so on) and only those with an interesting (and verifiable) history—that is, I needed to know who had bought the watch or who had been presented with it and why, and to have as much information as possible about the owner. As a final hurdle, I needed to be sure that the watch was in good mechanical condition and capable of being restored to keep time as accurately as it had when it left the workshops of Patek Philippe.

If all of these factors were present, I was interested, but even then there had to be something special and appealing about the watch to my eye, an elegance in the design, the dial, the hands, and the casing that caught my attention and that would make me happy every time I picked it up to see what the time was—which, I assume, was the case with many of the original owners of these watches.

I limit myself to about a dozen watches, which doesn't seem many when compared to the *hundreds* in other people's collections, but then the research on the ownership and history of my collection is a never-ending task, though pleasurable and interesting.

A watch should keep good time, of course, but it should also make you happy. Looking at it should make you feel better about yourself and the world, in however small a degree.

2
The Marketplace

*O*F COURSE, there's no law that says you have to buy watches at auctions, however famous and well established the auction houses. Some people love auctions; other people are intimidated by them. For some reason, I have never had good luck at auctions in buying anything, from livestock (pigs) to furniture. Stage fright, or something similar, seems to come over me, and I end up either buying something I don't want for more than I wanted to spend or breaking some unwritten rule of auction behavior and receiving a humiliating lecture from the auctioneer. I'm not just talking about big, elegant auctions, either, with men in power suits and women in designer clothes sitting around on spindly little gilt chairs holding little numbered plaques like funeral parlor fans to make their bids. I freeze even at Saturday night, small-town, country auctions, where people are bidding in $5 increments for an old card table or a set of garden furniture, and everybody is dressed in blue jeans.

When I started out collecting watches, I avoided auctions, but I soon learned that whether one went the auction route or not, the most valuable resource around for the beginning collector are the auction *catalogs*. These catalogs, lovingly and expensively produced by every major auction house, are prepared before every auction and usually can be ordered from the auction house for a fairly modest amount of money (it's their way of tempting you to make a bid, after all). Read carefully, with real attention, they constitute something like a home education course in watch collecting.

The major auction houses pay the world's leading experts to provide exact technical and historical descriptions of all the watches for sale, each of which is painstakingly photographed in full color, often with details of the movement. In addition, the auction catalogs are the quickest way of picking up the terms of the trade used to describe every watch—the name of the manufacturer, the date it was manufactured, the case material (yellow gold, white gold, pink gold, platinum, stainless steel, and so on), the fineness of the gold (18 karat, 14 karat, and so on), the type of the watch, whether simple or complicated (e.g., "Fine 18K yellow gold gentleman's wristwatch" or "Very fine two-tone platinum and gold keyless astronomical dress watch with perpetual calendar and phases of the moon and its age"), the exact details of the movement, the dimensions of the watch, and the distinguishing features of the dial and case. If the watch has a special history of any kind, there is likely to be a brief description of it and of the people involved, as well as, of course, an estimate of what it may fetch at auction. Some catalogs, most notably those of Antiquorum, also include a complex grading system for noting any flaws in the case, dial, hands, or movement.

Sometimes these catalogs will have a theme—marine and military watches, for example, or watches by a single manufacturer—and many of them group watches by the manufacturer. In short, the major auction houses have gone to a great deal of time and trouble to make their catalogs as visually attractive and informative as they can, and all you have to do is write to them to receive one; the charge for even the most elaborate catalogs is relatively modest, considering how much effort goes into them. What is more, these days much of the contents of each auction house's catalog is available on-line for nothing, as are the results of the auction, though in my view it's still worthwhile buying the catalogs and holding on to them, because they represent an invaluable reference source once they begin to accumulate.

My father was an inveterate collector of auction catalogs, and although he could not be trusted, in normal daily life, to remember to tie his shoelaces or put on socks of the same color, let alone wear a watch, he had an infallible memory for items he had seen on auction, sometimes decades before, and for auction prices too. He read his catalogs the way other people might read *The Racing Form* or a favorite magazine or book. Every room of his huge house in London was piled high with catalogs stacked against the wall or under the furniture. The latest ones were kept in his bathroom, so that he could go through them when he was least likely to be interrupted or bothered by people, carefully marking in pen items that caught his attention and turning a corner of the appropriate page down—it was before the age of Post-its, but my father would have loved them at first sight and instantly adapted them to his routine.

I was never able to discover what his filing system was, but there *was* one, even if it was only in his head. If somebody mentioned a bronze he had once admired at a sale at Spink's or Christie's years ago, my father would frown, go upstairs to one of the bedrooms or bathrooms, gaze for a few minutes at the seemingly endless stacks of identical catalogs, then pull out unerringly the one in which the bronze had last been offered on auction, usually with his notes beside it in the margins indicating who had bought it and at what price.

His routine on Saturday mornings was always the same— the auction rooms until about one o'clock, then a long, leisurely lunch with a couple of his auction-room cronies whose interests were similar to his own at a corner table at Prunier, off St. James's Street, or at the Hungarian Czardas on Dean Street, then home with his new acquisition (if it was portable) and a couple of refreshing hours to go through his auction catalogs some more until it was time for tea.

I was allowed to accompany him when I was a teenager, under strict instructions not to fidget or blink during the auction and to listen, not talk, during lunch. Because my father had a taste for almost every kind of objet d'art except watches, his cronies were a rum lot. One of them was a noted doctor; another was my grand-uncle Bert (on my mother's side of the family), a well-known antique dealer who dressed like a bookie, spoke impenetrable Cockney, and eventually ended up doing time at the age of eighty-four for burglarizing historic houses and selling their contents to rich Americans. Oddly enough, still another was the then Lord Chief Justice of England, a very old man, who shared with my father an interest in Renaissance bronzes. The Lord Chief Justice was the last of England's great "hanging judges," who apparently lived for those moments when a folded black silk square was placed on his long white wig and he condemned somebody to be hanged. My father once invited him home for dinner and a look at his collection of bronzes, but the Lord Chief Justice, though visibly tempted, shook his head regretfully. "I have observed over many years on the bench," he explained, "that whenever I particularly like a man and accept an invitation to his home, invariably I will sooner or later see him standing before me in the dock, waiting to be sentenced." Odder still, another crony was the hangman of England at the time, Mr. Pierrepoint, who collected eighteenth- and nineteenth-century engravings of famous hangings, which were on display at the Hanging Man, his pub across the river, along with the nooses he had used on some of his more famous victims.

My father's taste for eccentrics was one of his most endearing traits. He did not seek them out particularly; they simply attached themselves to him like flies to fly paper, and he always met them in the auction rooms. It caught my eye that the Lord Chief Justice and Mr. Pierrepoint both wore watch chains like my grandfather's across their waistcoat, the former a Prince Albert of heavy gold links, the latter a more modest silver one with a Masonic fob.

It should be noted first of all that by the time I began to accompany my father on Saturdays, I had already developed an eye for watches and their accoutrements, perhaps because it was the one subject about which my father knew little and cared less, and, second, I had already learned from his example that the most interesting people anybody was likely to meet in life are those who share one's own passion for a particular kind of collecting, whether it's old china or Master paintings or watches.

Over the years, I've come to understand and appreciate my father's Saturday mornings. I know plenty of people with whom I can spend long, tranquil, deeply engrossing hours talking about watches (or guns or World War II aircraft) over lunch or dinner with the greatest of pleasure, without ever learning anything at all about their wife or children or personal life, nor they of mine, and neither of us being in the slightest curious about any of that. Some of them, truth to tell, looked at objectively, are pretty odd ducks, who tend to have glittering wild eyes behind thick spectacle lenses and a fixed, monomaniacal expression. My wife Margaret, on the rare occasions she meets one of them, will say, "I can't imagine what you *see* in him!"—but then, she isn't a collector and doesn't understand that bond.

There is a great deal of pleasure to be had in those friendships that come from a shared interest in any subject, however esoteric—in a way, the more esoteric, the better— and watch collecting is no exception to the rule. Of course, people who are intently focused on one subject may sometimes seem odd in the clear, cold light of day (or of spousal judgment) but it's only among them that your interest in watches, or whatever it might be, is likely to find a receptive ear. Most other people, as you are quickly going to discover, will have only the most modest interest, if any at all, in your collection, let alone in hearing the details and provenance of each piece, together with the saga of your finding it. Only your fellow watch collectors are going to understand the thrill of discovering that an apparently ordinary pocket watch has, on close inspection, the last three digits of the serial number carefully engraved on each major component of the movement—a sign that it may have been made to compete in the annual timing trials at the Observatory of Geneva, in which points are awarded for the watch's accuracy in different positions, at extreme temperatures, and so on—or that an otherwise ordinary-looking stainless steel wristwatch has a broad arrow stamped on the back and an inventory number, signifying that it was bought for the British armed forces. Watch collectors delight in just such small details, most of which would escape the average person, who might pick up a rare and valuable item and say, out of politeness, "Pretty nice watch," without understanding just how unique and special it may be to the collector. With fellow collectors, I am never bored, and so far as I can tell, they are never bored by me, so long as I stick to the subject of watches.

Like all other forms of collecting, watch collecting has no end once you start. Just as book collectors never have enough books, watch collectors are always looking for that one elusive piece to round out their collection or discovering an interest in a whole new subset of watches or deciding to get rid of everything they have and start all over again in a new direction. Just as they seem to be getting toward their goal, whatever it may be, they have a way of losing interest. "Well, yes," somebody will say of a fellow collector, "he *was* putting together a pretty good Vacheron & Constantin collection, but then he sold it all off and started to collect Cartier watches from the 1920s instead."

This tendency to change goals just as you've built up a pretty good collection is one of the many reasons why the same watches keep showing up again and again in auction catalogs, and, of course, another reason why you should study auction catalogs with care. Watch collectors as a group seem rather more inclined to change horses in midstream than are, say, stamp collectors or gun collectors, but that's partly because many of them take up watch collecting before they've really developed an aesthetic sense of what they like or decided on a single unifying theme for their collection.

Anyway, the question of *how* to start collecting is in part dependent on where you live. Once you've got a fix on the kind of thing you want to collect, there's hardly a city in America that doesn't have one or more shops that sell and trade vintage watches. In fact, I'm constantly astonished, whenever I travel, by the number of places in even quite small towns that seem to specialize in vintage watches, and by the sheer quantity of watches available out there to buy. In some areas, they just seem to proliferate (southern Florida is one example, maybe because of the number of old people there who cling to their watches until the last moment), but hardly anywhere are watches hard to find. Of course, much of what such places have is junk, but that's true of other kinds of collecting, too, and, anyway, there's a certain satisfaction to looking through a lot of junk and finding that one piece that *is* interesting and perhaps even valuable, as you would know from reading all those auction catalogs carefully.

Many jewelry stores that sell estate jewelry will have interesting old watches—though once again, you have to have a sense for what you're looking for and how much it's worth. Perhaps most interesting of all are watch and jewelry shows, which bring hundreds, sometimes thousands, of vendors together in one place for one or more days (there's a big one in Miami, and others in Detroit or Orlando, but almost every big city has one at some point in the year). These are places where the serendipitous purchase *does* sometimes happen.

A friend of mine was recently walking through one of these shows, in the ballroom of a big hotel, with a man who collects enameled pocket watches—pieces with an enamel painting on the back or the cover. They are usually from the nineteenth century, but a very few of the top Swiss manufacturers still make them today as extremely rare and expensive *de luxe* items, mostly to demonstrate that there are still craftsmen who know how to do it, I suspect, and they have recently become a category in which prices are rising rapidly. While talking to my friend, the expert paused to look through a tray of pretty junky-looking old pocket watches, picked one up, examined it carefully, and bought it for $300 on the spot. It turned out to be an enameled Patek, which needed, it's true, some restoration and repair, but which he sold a year later on auction for $25,000.

Of course, that isn't going to happen often, and it isn't going to happen to you at all unless you have the expertise to know a good thing when you see it, but at these places it *does* happen, which isn't true of auctions or in transactions with an established professional dealer, who will usually have a pretty good idea of the value of everything in his stock and an eye trained to recognize quality under a layer of dirt, dust, and neglect.

Then there are private sales—individuals or collectors selling directly, either via the classified section of the local newspaper or, more frequently now, on the Internet. And then, of course, there are auctions.

It should be needless to point out that a lot can be said for *not* buying vintage watches from total strangers, or anything else, for that matter. Whenever possible, it is preferable to find somebody who deals in vintage watches *professionally.* Getting cheated in the vintage watch business is not any more or less difficult than in any other form of collecting. Leica collectors, for example, place a great value on cameras that were once Luftwaffe property, but judging from the number of Luftwaffe Leicas that come up for sale, either the Luftwaffe had more Leicas than they had aircraft, or somewhere in Europe a number of skilled craftsmen know how to spray the metal parts of the camera gray-blue, engrave the right markings, change the serial number, and give the whole thing a nice patina of wear and tear, thus transforming a camera worth perhaps hundreds of dollars into one worth thousands. The latter proposition seems more likely. Watches are relatively easy to fake, at least so far as the case and dial are concerned, and it's not insuperably difficult for somebody who knows what he's doing to convert a comparatively ordinary watch into one that has more desirable features. Rolex dials and hands, for example, are easy enough to change for somebody with the skill to do it, and can turn a watch that's of no great interest into a much more valuable and special one to the eyes of a beginner: the very popular early Rolex "Paul Newman Daytona" wrist chronographs in stainless steel, for example, are watches that require an expert to distinguish the real thing from an artful and well-executed fake.

Here again, if you've been looking through the auction catalogs, you'll at least have a sense for what the piece *ought* to look like and something against which to compare what's being offered to you, but of course your best bet still is to buy from somebody who has been in business for a while, knows a lot about watches, and has a reputation to protect.

At the very least, you then stand a chance of getting your money back if there's a problem.

Bear in mind, too, that short of becoming an experienced watchmaker yourself, it's very hard for an amateur to determine the *condition* of the movement. A certain amount of it may be clear from a good long look at it with a jeweler's loupe or a magnifying glass—the presence of dust and dirt need not be serious and may be taken care of with a good cleaning by a reputable watch repairman, but rust or marks and scratches on screw heads or on the plates close to screw heads, may be taken as evidence of careless treatment in the first case and of careless repair in the second. The fact that the watch doesn't run may not be significant if it's an old one, because these things can usually be repaired, but if the hands or the winding stem are immovably frozen, or if there is evidence of significant rust, then there may be big and expensive repair bills to come.

My own worst decisions in the field of watch collecting have always been buying a watch I like that has significant mechanical problems in the expectation that they can be fixed. I recall buying, at what seemed like a reasonable price, a beautiful Patek Philippe chronometer with a power reserve indicator (or "up-down" dial, which indicates how many hours the watch has yet to run, an obviously important feature on a chronometer intended as a subsidiary navigational device) on auction in Switzerland—a watch that I had always dreamed of owning. Big and very handsome, it was made around 1900 and had a rare and desirable "Extra" movement, which signifies that special care had been taken in assembling and finishing it. There were also the desirable facts that it scored third in the 1911–1912 Observatory of Geneva timing contest, a very high rating when one considers that hundreds of individual watches were submitted and tested, and that it was possible to trace the original owner and the jewelry store he had bought it from (a very important point for me), as well as the thick sheaf of papers in immaculate Swiss handwriting from the timing test. It "needed some work," I was told by somebody who examined the watch for me before the auction, but really, what did that matter, I thought, in view of its special appeal?

But, in the end, no amount of work could make the watch keep time as accurately as it had in 1911, and after putting into the restoration of the watch almost as much as I had spent to buy it, I eventually sold it. For me, the watch was no pleasure unless it kept good time—no watch ever is, in fact— but the person who bought the watch from me wanted it because it was a rare and beautiful piece that filled a hole in his collection; he had no intention of wearing it or, most likely, even of *winding* it. I didn't lose any money in the end, but the experience taught me a lesson that I've followed ever since in collecting, which is never to ignore what is important to *you,* however odd or unimportant it may seem to other people. No matter how desirable the piece is, if it can't keep perfect time, I don't want it. Nor do I want to enter into open-ended jobs of repair and restoration, which can cost a fortune and still not produce a watch that runs perfectly.

Others obsess about exterior condition—even the faintest suggestion of a scratch or a ding on the case is enough to put them off; the watch has to look like new, even if it's a hundred years old. Still others, (and they are the most interesting collectors of all) consider the condition of the watch or its ability to run accurately secondary to its importance as an object that fills a hole or a slot in some grand design: a history of the development of certain kinds of movements, or the complete range of a certain manufacturer's products, and so on. Visitors to the American Clock and Watch Museum in Bristol, Connecticut, can get some idea of this approach easily enough.

I had not realized that the museum even existed until a friend, distinguished vintage watch dealer and jeweler Edward Faber, pointed it out to me and mentioned that a watch collectors' organization was arranging for a special, guided tour of it. Though I'm not usually one for clubbish outings, I made up my mind to try it, though I decided to forego the bus trip and the lunch and to drive there in my own car.

The reason why the museum is in Bristol—a question I asked myself several times during what seemed like an interminably long drive from our farm in upstate New York—is that this town used to be the center of Connecticut's thriving clock and watch business. Once upon a time, the entire area around Bristol was dotted with factories turning out a vast range of timepieces, from "dollar" watches to elaborate "cased" clocks, that sold in huge quantities all over the world. That industry simply vanished after World War II as other countries with cheaper labor began to take over the marketplace for inexpensive, mass-produced timepieces; then, cheap quartz watches and digital watches flooded in—the *coup de grace*. Bristol had once been a thriving city of red-brick watch and clock "manufacturies," now mostly abandoned or put to other uses, as well as home to the craftsmen who provided the labor, but nothing of that remains now except the museum, which is modestly contained in a handsome old eighteenth century house, shaded by big trees.

One look at the fellow members of my tour as I joined them confirmed the wisdom of my decision to travel independently. Several of them had the look of people afflicted with some form of obsessional fixation—what my son Christopher would call "the mad scientist look," with buttons buttoned in the wrong buttonholes and wild hair; others seemed enormously old, and still others were clearly retired watchmakers, with the characteristic stooped back and pale complexion of those who have spent a lifetime hunched over a workbench dealing with pieces hardly larger than a period in this book, many bearing an impressive array of magnifying spectacles on their nose. Their range of knowledge about clocks, watches, and timekeeping was overwhelming, and their thirst for detail unquenchable. I was, frankly, out of my depth and for the first time in many years found myself being addressed as "young man."

Over the years since its foundation, the museum has been the beneficiary of many personal collections, with the result that it has a bewildering amount of material on display, some of it extraordinary, some of it a tribute to the eccentric interests of collectors. When it comes to "long" or "cased" clocks—what are commonly called "grandfather clocks" by the hoi polloi—the museum has room after room of them, densely packed one against the other, many of them exquisite. I found that my interest in long clocks was satiated long before that of the rest of the members of my tour, however, and was therefore wool-gathering and half-asleep on my feet (not difficult to do when surrounded by hundreds of clocks ticking away) when I heard our guide point out that a number of these clocks had movements in which all the pieces—gears, wheels, levers and so forth—were carved out of wood.

I came to with a start. The idea of *wooden* clockworks had never occurred to me, though clearly the other members of my tour, who were nodding wisely, knew all about them. I prowled around and soon found that there was, as usual, a perfectly sound reason for making the mechanism of a clock out of wood. Before the American Revolution, Great Britain made certain that metal clockworks and clock parts had to be imported into the colonies, like most "manufactured" goods, and that, plus the fact that the colonies lacked industralization, made it necessary for them to "buy British." Thus, because there was in America an inexhaustible supply of wood and no great shortage of men who spent a good part of their lives whittling wood with a penknife, the idea of a clock with wooden parts came about fairly naturally. Moreover, these clocks worked. Several of them were still keeping accurate time right in front of my eyes in Bristol, Connecticut, more than two hundred years later—what is more, given the self-lubricating properties of certain kinds of wood, the clocks needed less care than normal ones and made less noise as they ticked.

What fascinated me was that the wooden clocks had been collected mostly by a single man, who must obviously have spent the best part of his lifetime amassing them. Where he found the space to store them was a puzzle, too—he must have had not only plenty of it, but a very understanding wife, because each and every one of the clocks was tall and a massive dust collector. He also managed to find pocket watches in which all the parts were carved out of different kinds of wood, the creations of Russian wood carvers in the nineteenth century, who had time on their hands during the long winters and no easy access to metal parts. Even

Russian wooden watch, with carved wooden box and wooden chain.
(Photo by Antiquorum)

the watch *chains* were intricately fabricated out of perfectly carved wooden links. (For a time in nineteenth-century Russia, I learned, wooden watches were briefly fashionable as curiosities among the rich and titled, representing as they did an authentically *Russian* way of measuring time, as opposed to an imported Swiss watch.)

I cannot say that I was instantly tempted to rush out and start collecting wooden clocks or watches—even the watches, in their polished wood cases, are bulky and have a certain "homespun" look to them that is not my cup of tea—but I was significantly impressed by the way in which one man had effectively built up a collection with a unique focus and, presumably, made himself an expert on the subject. In the final analysis, I thought, that's what really matters: focus, commitment to an idea or brand or type of watch, and knowledge.

I staggered out of the museum reeling from the sheer quantity and diversity of the exhibits, ranging in size from a giant clockworks designed for a steeple or public building that is at least two stories high and more like a Victorian steam engine than a clock, to tiny mass-manufactured parts that can be seen properly only through a magnifying glass. What is amazing is not that all this diversity has been gathered in a museum—there are much stranger museums in this country: think of the John Nance Garner Museum in Uvalde, Texas, for example, with its unique collection of presentation gavels, surely the largest in the world—but that so many people over the years have collected such highly specialized material with such fierce energy and total commitment: collections of springs, collections of watch parts, collections of movements, collections of watchmaking machinery. Everywhere there is evidence not only of the relentless need to collect, but of the even greater need to collate, compare, file, and instruct. There is a didactic quality to most of the material, a determined effort to explain by what stages a part or a piece of a movement was made or how a certain kind of movement developed over time. The museum is here to instruct rather than to amuse, which may explain the comparatively small number of children there.

The chief thing I brought away from it myself, however, was the realization that no matter how specialized and esoteric an object is in the world of clocks and watches, there is sure to be *somebody* out there collecting it. Carriage clocks (those little rectangular clocks that people took with them on a journey in the early nineteenth century), American-made alarm clocks, time clocks for factories and offices, marine chronometers, Boy Scout watches, triangular Masonic pocket watches—you name it, somebody out there has put his or her heart and soul into becoming the Master of that particular tiny segment of the Universe of Time.

One thing is clear: money shouldn't be the sole or major issue when you set out to form a collection. Many people are prevented from collecting by the thought of what it will cost—and, of course, cost will always be a consideration for all except those who would rather let their children starve and wear shoes with holes in the soles and run-down heels than forego owning the watch of their dreams. Watch collecting produces plenty of people who fall into the latter category, though not necessarily by design, but it's not the right way to approach building up a collection. In the first place, it is possible to have a very good and even unique collection of watches and still remain within relatively modest spending limits. There are all sorts of interesting areas in which to collect that don't involve you in paying high six figures for a coveted wristwatch or seven figures for a landmark *grandes complications* pocket watch.

One of the most expensive wristwatches ever sold on auction, a 1938 Patek Philippe astronomic, rectangular, curved platinum gentleman's wristwatch, with triple date calendar à guichets and moon phases, the only one of its kind known to exist.
(Photo by Antiquorum)

It's like collecting anything else: if you follow your eye and your interest, you can build up a nice collection of paintings without necessarily going after works by Van Gogh or Turner for tens of millions of dollars. Having some idea of what you're looking for is more important than having a lot of money to spend. The urge to acquire is not the same as the urge to *collect:* the latter presupposes some coherent theme and the self-discipline to stick to it, whereas the former may mean nothing more than buying a whole lot of watches that have nothing in common except high price or big brand names.

When I was at school in Switzerland, one of the big innovations in watchmaking was a wristwatch called the "Cricket," *with an alarm,* made by Vulcan, a rather inexpensive watchmaker with a taste for what were, by the standards of the day, rather futuristic dials in many variations. These watches were so popular that almost every pupil at Le Rosey had a "Cricket." Unlike an alarm clock, they had a wide variation of rings, and the result was that from all over the school we could hear them chirping, squeaking, chiming, and buzzing on people's wrists from about 6:00 to 6:30 every morning, as if a giant nest of insects had been disturbed in its sleep. Some of these watches were handsome pieces of art deco design—in the Rockefeller Center tradition of modern design—and would not have looked out of place at the 1939 World's Fair; they turn up from time to time at auctions and at watch and jewelry shows. I've never seen one go for more than a few hundred dollars, even in gold, but it's often occurred to me that they would be an interesting and rewarding thing to collect and that, given the number of variations, you could probably end up with a sizeable collection of unusual (and very wearable) "Cricket" wristwatches.

The same thing can be said of Bulova Accutron electronic watches, which came in many futuristic and handsome
designs and in an enormous variety of styles, and which were
once the rage. Cornelius Ryan, author of *The Longest Day,*
was the very proud owner of one of the first Accutrons made;
it was transparent, so you could see the electronic heart of the
watch through the dial and the back, like a skeleton watch,
and was then regarded as if it were the Eighth Wonder of the
World—a watch that ran on a battery, never needed to be
wound up, didn't tick, and kept perfect time, with a discreet
electric hum. Most of the Accutrons looked as if they had
been designed by Raymond Loewy, and perhaps in fact they
were. In any event, they were widely believed at the time to
be sounding the death knell for the Swiss watch industry.
Who would want to wind a watch or depend on a clumsy,
mechanical self-winding watch when they could have an
Accutron humming away on their wrist?

As it turned out, the Accutron, like the even more radical
and modernistic Pulsar (the first popular "digital" watch), was
an expensive curiosity or novelty that never really caught on
or, at any rate, didn't catch on enough to worry the Swiss or
save the American watch industry. Within a few years, the
introduction of the cheap quartz movement for conventional-
looking watches and the flood of cheap quartz and digital
watches from Asia rendered the Accutron superfluous, but
there are still quite a few of them around, and prices have been
going steadily upward, which means that it may be too late to
get on the bandwagon. Still, the point remains valid—here is
another subarea of watchmaking in which it would have been
possible, up to a few years ago, to build up a fascinating collection for a comparatively small investment, as well as a watch

(and a brand name in American watchmaking) that would certainly be worth learning about. Nor would collecting it have been an insuperably difficult task. Bulova is still in business; their corporate records exist; whole books have been written about the watch; plenty of owners are still alive and breathing; and the time is about right for the curious art deco style of most of the designs to have become fashionable again. The Accutron not only remains an interesting and major step in American watchmaking, but is also a watch that you can still wear today—accurate, reliable, and of striking appearance.

My point is that here are two areas in which collecting would have been rewarding and interesting without being exorbitantly expensive. Anybody perusing the catalogs of Christie's, Sotheby, Antiquorum, or Phillips could find a dozen more possibilities.

Take, for example, Vacheron & Constantin. During the nineteenth century, it was a brand name that rivaled Patek Philippe, one of the two or three most distinguished and inventive of Swiss firms, patronized by royalty and celebrities. This remained true until shortly after World War II, when Patek pulled far ahead of Vacheron & Constantin in snob appeal, price, value, and originality of design, with the result that nineteenth-century Vacheron pocket watches, some of the most beautiful and complicated watches ever made, sell for a fraction of the cost of a comparable Patek, even when they are in perfect condition, with the original box and paperwork. The Vacheron & Constantin "Chronomètres Royales" are, for example, by any standards, watches of great beauty and distinction. The workmanship of the cases and movements are up to the very highest standards, but such has been the glamour of the Patek Philippe name over the past fifty years or so in terms of contemporary watches that it put the older Vacheron & Constantin products in the shade so far as prices are concerned—not that they're exactly *cheap,* but they're a fraction of what a similar Patek Philippe would cost and, in view of their quality, often underpriced.

Audemars Piguet, another of the great names of Swiss watchmaking, was in the early twentieth century every bit as respected as Patek and Vacheron & Constantin, and indeed was famous for their watches *de très grande complication,* which even today are of exquisite complexity and beauty. From time to time, in fact, in the small, interlocking world of Swiss watchmaking firms, Audemars Piguet actually produced components and even completed movements for Patek, but the company never acquired the same prestige and fame abroad, and the price of their watches on auction has never equaled that of comparable Patek watches (though they're beginning to rise and catch up now, so you may have let this one wait until too late). Once again, this is the area in which a great collection could have been made, built around the watches of a single marque.

For years, the nineteenth- and early-twentieth-century pocket watches of the German manufacturer A. Lange & Söhne could be bought in stunning condition for relatively modest prices. They were—and remain—superb watches, originally intended to prove that anything the Swiss could do, the Germans could do better, or at least as well. Though not always as gracefully designed as the very best Swiss watches of the period, they were handsome, beautifully finished, very ambitious in terms of complications offered, and, of course, outstandingly accurate. Lange was not necessarily a name to conjure with outside Germany, except to experts.

A late-nineteenth-century A. Lange & Söhne hunter pocket watch.
(Photo courtesy Phillips, de Pury & Luxembourg)

Then, a decade or so ago, revived since the war, it came out with a series of unusual, very expensive, and quite unique wristwatches that quickly made the name famous in the more expensive jewelry stores. The Lange wristwatch, with its elegant, large dial, its outsize date indicator, and its power reserve indicator, became a power symbol and fashion statement for men. As a result, the old Lange pocket watches leapt up in price, particularly since German collectors wanted a wide range of their nineteenth-century products now that it was permissible again for Germans to feel a certain chauvinistic pride in German precision workmanship.

The prices of Lange watches are rising swiftly, but it would have been possible to have built up a collection of superb and often unique watches at relatively modest prices had one been watching the marketplace carefully only a few years ago. What's more, the attention paid to the old Lange pocket watches has pushed new and collectible Langes up into the watch stratosphere—their platinum "Pour le

Mérite" wristwatch (with a tourbillon), only fifty examples of which were made, in 1991, sells for upwards of $150,000 as I write.

A word is perhaps in order about watches and money. Many people are under the impression that collector watches are "a hedge against inflation" and a good investment; historically there is certainly some truth to this belief. As the stock market continues to falter and fall as I write, watches certainly look like a better investment than, say, a wide range of NASDAQ stocks, but then what doesn't? Good watches *do* tend to hold their value even during a period of financial chaos, but buying watches as a kind of investment portfolio requires an acute sense of what is likely to hold or increase its value and what is not. True, prices have never crashed in the watch market, as they did with vintage and collector cars in the 1990s, when Ferrari Californias that had been selling for $3 million or $4 million suddenly plummeted to under $1 million and don't look like they'll be coming up again any time in the near future. With a few exceptions, however, the prices of collector watches haven't taken off like a rocket, but they *have* gone steadily up over the years.

Whether it's a good idea to think of watch collecting primarily as an investment is another question. In the first place, I'm not sure that's ever the best reason to go about building up a collection of *anything*—a collection should give the collector pleasure first and foremost, and if it increases in value, so much the better. The basic mathematics of watch collecting should be kept firmly in mind: if you buy an item at an auction, you will pay a fee to the auction house of something like 10 to 20 percent of your successful bid; if you buy from a dealer in vintage watches, it is of course harder to know what his markup and profit on a given piece is, but it's hardly likely to be less than that of an auction house if he is going to stay in business. Essentially this means that if you buy a piece on auction for $1,000, it will cost you at least $1,100 to walk out of the auction house with it, while if a dealer buys a piece from somebody for $1,000, he is going to charge you at least $1,500 (plus the prevailing local sales tax) for it. Thus, depending on where you bought it, the value of the piece is going to have to *increase* by at least 10 to 50 percent before you even *break even* on your purchase. Hence, buying watches with investment in mind is a long-term business, not the equivalent of day trading.

What is more, as with many things, the harsh reality is that "you buy retail, you sell wholesale," so the value of the item in the marketplace has to erase that gap before you can make a penny of a profit out of selling it. Of course, to dedicated collectors none of this matters, in part because their first concern is buying what they like or want—the idea that it's a good investment may be something they tell their wives or themselves or sometimes they simply want to believe because it makes them feel better about spending the money—and in part because they usually live in a constant drama of buying and selling pieces, or trading a piece they've decided they *don't* want in partial payment for a piece they've fallen in love with, so they're never sure of the total value of their collection and probably won't find out in the real world until, for one reason or another, they decide to sell out and collect something else. Either that, or their heirs will find out when *they* come to sell the collection, often to their surprise or dismay.

Any way you look at it, for most people collecting watches is a hobby, perhaps a passion, but not necessarily a sound investment scheme. For one thing, prices are not as firmly established as they are in, say, stamp collecting or coin collecting, and, for another, the object itself is far more idiosyncratic and personal in appeal than a stamp or a coin. The aesthetics, the design, and the history of a given watch have to please *you* before you buy it. In the end, collecting what you really like, know, understand, and are curious about, not only is more rewarding in terms of the experience itself, but probably will prove more rewarding financially over the long run.

If I mention all this, it's because it pays to go into watch collecting with a clear mind about it and to learn as much as you can right at the beginning, rather than over the years by trial and error and by personal (and often expensive) experience, like most of us. The marketplace, like the marketplace for all collectibles from antique furniture to first editions, is amorphous, ranging from individuals with an "interesting" timepiece in their pocket to established dealers and the big auction houses of the world. The neophyte collector's first reaction to it all is to be dazzled by the sheer diversity and glamour of what's for sale and thus to want to own it all. This attitude is bound to cost you money, so it helps to do three basic things before getting out your checkbook or platinum credit card.

First of all, *learn* something about watches—at any rate, enough to figure out what you like and what kind of collection you'd like to have. Try to figure out what interests you and what form your collection might take *before* going on a buying spree. Second, dip your toe in the water *without* buying—read the auction catalogs, attend auctions, study the prices at the end of the sale, paying special attention to objects that sold for far more or far less than you (or the auction house) estimated; go to shows and shops, talk to dealers—most of them are happy to talk watches with anybody, provided you pick a moment when they're not busy making a sale. Third, read as much as you can about watches so that you have at least a working familiarity with the various brands, types, and styles of watch, both old and new, and some idea of what makes certain watches or certain movements "special" in terms of interest and value.

In fact, almost the best thing you can do before starting to collect watches is to take a deep breath, calm down, and start reading. There are specialized books on almost every major brand and marque, some of them quite elaborate (I am not a Rolex collector, but I have at least three huge and well-illustrated histories of Rolex on my shelf, and I would think twice before getting into collecting Rolex watches without reading them). There are even more specialized books on identifying and pricing watches; before you wade in to start collecting American pocket watches, for example, it would be sensible to read something like *American Pocket Watches: Identification and Price Guide,* by Roy Ehrhardt and James L. Hernick. And finally, there are magazines devoted to watches and societies of watch collectors. In short, a great deal of information is out there in books and magazines—and more still on the Web—some of it free, and all of it a lot cheaper than buying a watch, let alone learning later that the watch you've bought isn't what you thought it was or worth what you paid for it.

In any case, the watches are out there—in vast quantities, in every possible quality and type, and in an infinity of divergent forms and complications. The question is how to get started on your own collection of humankind's most ubiquitous and widespread invention.

Choosing What to Collect:
"Vintage" or "Collectible"?

ANYBODY LOOKING through an auction catalog will notice at once that almost every watch out of the hundreds described in detail therein is described as "Very fine and rare" or "Very fine and extremely rare." No watch is ever described as "Ordinary and not particularly rare"—words apparently excluded from the vocabulary of auctioneering.

A second thing you will notice is that a very large number of the watches for sale—quite often the majority, in fact—are either pretty ordinary older watches or brand new watches, exactly the same as those you might buy from a watch store. Admittedly, some of the latter are certainly *expensive* watches, sometimes even *very* expensive ones, but they are still identical to ones that you could buy, if you were rich enough, at Tourneau in New York City or at Tiffany & Co. or at glamorous watch and jewelry stores throughout the world (including the duty-free shops of the great airports). This is a phenomenon that should give the potential collector a moment's pause.

The watch business has always covered itself with the fig leaf of fixed retail prices, as have most jewelry stores. Until a few years ago, if the list price of a watch was, say, $4,000, you expected to write out a check for $4,000, plus sales tax, for the watch. But as the list price of prestigious watches escalated and potential customers began to wonder why they couldn't bargain for a deal, as they did when buying a car or a camera, this starchy facade began to collapse, though with as little fanfare as possible. The first big change was when the larger watch shops began to offer the customer a trade-in on their present watch—a tactic borrowed directly from the automobile business. Then gradually it became common practice to discount new watches. Of course, you couldn't expect to walk into Cartier or Tiffany and bargain for a watch as if you were in an Arab souk or an American car dealership—if a Cartier watch was listed at $10,000, anybody who walked in off Fifth Avenue and said, "I'll give you $7,500, you take my old watch and forget about the sales tax," would very likely be politely but firmly shown to the door. However, even in many of the stuffier and more elegant shops, customers who were known to the management were emphatically *not* shown to the door when they asked for a deal. On the contrary, they got it, and the practice quickly spread, until soon there were two standards of pricing in the retail watch business (as there are in the high-end retail camera business or car business), the price for the schmucks and the price for people who knew how to strike a hard bargain and who merely laugh when they are quoted the list price for an item.

This change in practice had two consequences. One was that a way had to be found to sell at reasonable prices perfectly good watches that had been taken as trade-ins, without their winding up in pawn shops or the equivalent and thereby debasing the brand names. The other was that a secondary market grew for expensive watches that simply couldn't be sold at the manufacturer's list price, which was always kept artificially high.

In addition, a whole new set of factors on the global level began to affect the high-end watch market. Chief among these factors was the rise and fall of currencies and of economies. For example, when the Thai economy was booming and the Thai bhat was riding high as a currency, the jewelers of Bangkok could and did stock up on high-end Rolexes and Patek Philippes, and were sure of selling them— in every culture, one of the first things people do when they make a lot of money is to buy and flaunt an expensive watch— but when the Thai economy faltered and the bhat plunged, the jewelers naturally found themselves with a lot of hugely expensive stock on their hands and no customers. These watches—brand-new, still sealed in their shipping cartons— made their way back to places where the economy was still healthy (until recently, first and foremost the United States), but at much lower wholesale prices than those set by the manufacturer in Switzerland. What is more, a purchaser with dollars (or Deutschmarks, or, for a time, yen) would benefit hugely from the rapidly falling value of the Thai currency. With a relatively modest investment of dollars, a dealer could

buy expensive high-end Swiss watches from overstocked jewelers in places such as Thailand, Indonesia, and most of the
countries of Latin America as their economies and currencies
went over the brink, taking the jewelers with them. The stu-
pendous advances in communication speeded up this process.
If the dealer had a customer who was looking for a fairly rare
and expensive item—say, a Patek Philippe wrist chronograph
with perpetual calendar and moon phases in platinum that
might retail for something like $250,000 or more—he or she
could get on the FAX machine or e-mail, locate one at the
best possible price halfway around the world, and get it by
Federal Express two days later.

Thus, for a number of reasons, the supply of high-end
watches increased rapidly in the 1980s and 1990s, at prices
that were significantly lower than the listed U.S. retail prices,
and the number of places where you could buy such watches
was no longer restricted to the better jewelry and watch
stores. Of course, there was nothing to *prevent* someone from
walking into Cartier on Fifth Avenue and buying a Cartier
"Pasha" wristwatch for the retail price plus sales tax, but that
person could buy exactly the same watch, brand-new, still in
the original sealed shipping box, for a fraction of the price
around the corner at many shops that sold watches on the
secondary market or at major auctions; the only thing the
purchaser *wouldn't* get was Cartier's gift wrapping, but at a
saving of $10,000 or more on a $30,000 watch he or she
might not have minded that too much.

Although the watch industry—especially the more prestigious Swiss firms—never got around to admitting that their
products were being discounted and did their best to ignore
the whole sordid business for as long as possible, the fact

remains that during the past ten or twenty years everybody *knew* that the retail price of expensive watches was becoming as flexible as the retail price of expensive cars, except for those few models that were in such demand or in such short supply that they always went for the full retail price or more.

A second phenomenon also affected the Swiss watch industry during the past twenty years or so. Up until the 1960s or the 1970s, nobody paid much attention to watch collectors, who tended to be eccentrics pursuing special interests in the area of vintage or unusual timepieces. Then, as the whole business of collectibles began to take off with a bang, watches became a hot area of collecting. One result was that some of the more desirable older watches quite suddenly became more valuable than new ones. To take a fairly

Rolex watches from the 1930s. Note the fascinating dials, particularly the second watch from the left, in which the hour appears in a small window at the top.
(Photo by Antiquorum)

typical example, a Rolex watch of the 1920s or 1930s began to sell for far more than a *new* Rolex: in some cases, the used, older versions of a model that was still being produced, such as the Submariner or the Daytona, fetched far higher prices than a brand-new version of the same model.

On one level, of course, the watch manufacturers were pleased enough that their old products were becoming chic and increasing rapidly in value, because some of that glamour rubbed off on the new models, but on another level they were dismayed that none of the increase in the value of older watches was going into their pockets.

No doubt it was satisfying to sit in Geneva and read that a Patek Philippe Calatrava wristwatch made in the 1930s had sold on auction for far more than the price of a new Calatrava wristwatch at a jewelry store, but the profit was going to auction galleries and vintage watch dealers, not to Patek. This is always a source of angst to corporations. When the prices of used Ferraris began to soar above those of new Ferraris, Commendatore Ferrari was anything but pleased. In the first place, he was interested in his *new* cars, not in the old ones, however glamorous people found them; indeed, so small was his interest in the old ones that at the Ferrari factory outside Modena rare and valuable prototypes were left to rust outside on the junk heap, while the factory got on with the more important business of manufacturing new Ferraris. In the second place, the soaring prices of old Ferraris, as collectors bought them up as "classics," didn't put a penny in the Commendatore's pockets, unlike the sale of a new one. The profit went to vintage car dealers, or to auction houses, not to Ferrari, with the result that the factory eventually began to make purchasers of some of the more exotic and rare later models such as the F-40 guarantee in writing that they would not sell the car for a year or more after they had taken delivery, in order to try and prevent the price of the car in the secondary market from immediately soaring far above the factory's price, and of course to discourage customers from buying a car only to sell it at a profit the next day.

The economics of collecting were there for the watch industry to contemplate, which was on the one hand tempting and on the other hand dangerous. The watch industry's central concern, after all, was not to cater to collectors, but to persuade people to buy expensive new watches and to keep their own production lines busy and their profits high. Eventually their response to the swift growth of collector interest was to capitalize on it by boldly producing collectibles—watches made in small numbers specifically to be collected with additional features and/or decoration, special packaging, and, very often, special serial numbers.

No doubt the example of companies such as Leitz, in the high-end camera business, served as a model for them. A small world of collectors had always hovered around the company's prestigious Leica camera, with the result that even before World War II some older "used" Leicas were worth more than a new one, but Leitz shrewdly set out to tap this collector market after the war by producing their own "limited edition" Leicas, intended specially for collectors, often commemorating an event or a personality in the history of photography. Internally, they were exactly the same camera that you could buy in any photo store that sold Leicas, but they bore special serial numbers, often a special finish (gold plated or titanium plated or black paint instead of matte chrome), an engraved logo to mark a special occasion, say, the five hundredth anniversary of Columbus's discovery of America, and were packed in a special rare-wood display case instead of in a normal shipping carton. What was soon very clear was that Leitz could sell five hundred or a thousand such cameras at $7,500 or more each, even though it was basically the same camera that a customer could buy for $1,500 in a store and cost about the same to manufacture. All the company had to do was tart it up a bit, give it a special run of serial numbers, and put it in a mahogany, velvet-lined box instead of a cardboard one. Commercially speaking, a "no brainer."

Gun manufacturers had led the way more than a century ago, as a matter of fact, by producing "limited," or "custom" versions of popular handguns, rifles, and shotguns. All they had to do, they learned, was give the weapon a better finish, add a little engraving and a better class of wood, maybe put a gold bead on the front sight, and pack it in a polished wooden display case, and they could double or triple the price of a gun they were already manufacturing anyway. So long as the numbers were kept low—ideally the manufacturer should produce *fewer* than the market could absorb so that the customer could sell his weapon for more than he paid for it—everybody was happy. Colt, Winchester, and Remington became experienced specialists in this field as early as the nineteenth century, and the example was therefore waiting around to be picked up by other industries in which there was a collector interest and a lively secondary market: high-end fountain pens, cameras, and, eventually, watches.

To understand all this is to understand the nature of what is out there to collect and why so much of it resembles, superficially at any rate, the same watches you can see at any *de luxe* watch shop, albeit at different prices. The watchmakers did not go into the business of making collectibles halfheartedly or on a small scale once they decided to go that route. Most of these "limited collectors' editions" are embellished in special ways, or they have unusual features or complications or unique dials and special serial numbers, and they are invariably packaged in lavish display cases instead of in the usual shipping carton (it's as if the Swiss watchmakers had paid a visit to Wetzlar to look at the Leitz factory and came away saying, "*Ja, ja,* we could do that also!"). Some manufacturers have ignored the collectible market altogether—Rolex, perhaps because Rolex's appeal is to sporty people and to the newly rich whose idea of class is a big gold Rolex on the wrist; and Patek because they have always taken the view that *every* Patek Philippe watch is a collector's item, that the whole *idea* of buying a Patek is to keep it for your lifetime and pass it on to your children, and they to theirs. It's perhaps for this reason, apart from the sheer luxury of the brand, that Patek watches tend to come in luxuriously designed cases, as suitable for display as for sticking away in a desk drawer. It's as if the good folks at Patek in Geneva were saying, "You can keep it as a cherished heirloom in the box or take it out, put it on, and wear it every day; it's entirely up to you." If you do the former, you'll be "collecting" it, if you do the latter you'll have the satisfaction of wearing an example of perhaps the most prestigious brand name in the watch industry, and it will probably go up in value anyway.

Of course, many of these collectibles aren't that much more valuable than their ordinary equivalents. It's a market to which close attention needs to be paid, if you're tempted by it, bearing in mind that objects that have been deliberately designed and manufactured to appeal to collectors are very seldom as valuable, over the long haul, as objects that have an intrinsic appeal in terms of design, history, ownership, or special quality that attracts collectors. Omega, for example, a medium-price Swiss watchmaker with a good reputation for well-made but perhaps not terribly exciting watches, makes a nice water-resistant stainless-steel chronograph called the Speedmaster Professional, which has always played second fiddle to Rolex's Daytona chronograph, though in many respects the Omega watch, being lighter, is easier to wear and—in my eyes, at any rate—more elegant and just as well made. When NASA was looking for a watch for the astronauts to wear on the first moon landing—a sudden, last-minute decision, nobody at NASA apparently having given any thought to the astronauts' need for a watch—they searched the Houston watch stores and came up with the Omega, which, because it was waterproof and about a third of the price of the comparable Rolex, seemed to fit the bill. Ever since, this model bears on its case back the engraved message, "THE FIRST WATCH WORN ON THE MOON—FLIGHT QUALIFIED FOR ALL NASA SPACE MISSIONS." Needless to say, though this model is exactly the same as other Omega chronographs without the NASA legend on the case back, it fetches a premium and is considered "more collectible."

The thing is not to mix apples and oranges. Almost any watch can be the basis for an extended collection if it's what attracts and interests you, but it is a good deal less expensive (and more fun) to develop your own interest in a given brand or type of watch and to go out looking for it than to buy watches that have been expensively designed to supply the need for a ready-made collection.

Choosing What to Collect

The vast bulk of the watches for sale out there can be conveniently divided into a relatively limited number of categories (naturally, some watches will overlap more than one category—there is simply no way to place precisely every watch in any system of categories).

1. "Vintage" watches that are of special interest because of their design, their manufacturer, the innovation of their movement, their complexity, or their history

2. "Collectible" watches that have been designed by and large to appeal to the collector and usually are distinguished by some significant element of design that makes the watch different from other watches by the same manufacturer

3. Watches of excellent or well-known manufacture that are relatively recent—usually "used" examples, in good condition, of the more popular brands and types of modern (post-World War II) watches

4. Watches of very special collector appeal—"military" watches would be one example, American "railroad" pocket watches of the nineteenth century another

5. Run of the mill "used" watches of lesser known manufacture (or unsigned) and ranging from mildly interesting or unusual to total junk

Oddly enough, category five is potentially the most interesting, because it is here that the great finds happen. Somebody with a skilled eye can very often spot a rare and unusual watch hidden in a drawer or display case full of undistinguished ones and end up buying for very little money a watch that will be worth a fortune once it has been cleaned up and its history traced.

Category four requires a special degree of discipline and a great deal of knowledge. You have to be able to keep on the straight and narrow of what you've set out to collect and need to know enough to recognize something special when you see it. It calls for lots of background research—there are many fakes.

Category three is perhaps the least interesting, but it offers an opportunity to buy watches that you admire for a fraction of what a new one would cost—bearing in mind that most modern watches are pretty indestructible and can be restored to like-new (or at any rate to working as good as new) by the manufacturer, who will usually still have parts for it.

Category two I dealt with previously. It can range from fairly ordinary watches to some of the most expensive and unusual modern wristwatches in the world.

Category one is where the big risks as well as the champagne and caviar come into play. Vintage watches—*genuinely* vintage—can range from inexpensive but respectable and interesting old watches to a one-of-a-kind wristwatch that may sell for $4 million or more or to a pocket watch of unique complexity and number of complications that sells for nearly three times that amount.

The great puzzles and mysteries of collecting are here, too, in this category—ancient watches with strange movements that proved to be dead ends in the history of horology; watches with a unique history of ownership, such as Marie Antoinette's famous Breguet, to take an extreme example; watches of great distinction whose pedigree still needs to be sorted out; watches that represented the very summit of design, elegance, and expensiveness when they were manufactured; watches that once belonged to famous (or notorious) people; watches that have a special historical interest; watches that somehow communicate something special to you when you pick them up.

Some watches in this category combine many different layers of interest. I am thinking, for example, of the platinum wristwatch presented by two Americans to Marshal Foch, *généralissmo* of the victorious Allied armies in 1918, which combines overwhelming beauty of design, a movement of interesting complexity for an early wristwatch, a high degree of historic interest, and undisputed provenance in the form of letters, documents, and so on. As somebody who is interested in World War I, I would have found this an irresistible item had I been able to afford it, as for different reasons I would have found irresistible a beautiful Vacheron & Constantin Chronomètre Royale, their handsome pocket chronometer of the late nineteenth and early twentieth centuries, which is a little too large in diameter for my taste, as a rule, but which in this example, had engraved on it the rays of a setting sun in exquisite, perfect proportions.

Naturally, pocket watches play a large part in category one, but a minor part in the other categories. For many reasons, pocket watches often run to greater complications (there's more room in the case for extra wheels, parts, springs, levers, jewels, gears, and gongs) and greater historical interest (there's more room on the inside and the outside of the case for long, elaborate inscriptions and fancy engraved or enameled initials or coats of arms).

Of course, you can mix and match, but sooner or later you're likely to become bored by a collection that has no common, defining theme. If what you want is a collection of modern "collectible" wristwatches, go for it, but even then it would be more interesting if you collected, say, all Audemars Piguet watches or Universal Geneve Tri-Compax chronographs, or aviator watches (you could build up a pretty varied collection just collecting Breitling aviator watches, which come in a wide variety of models, much modified over the years.) What's more, because these watches are pretty sturdy, you could wear them every day without too much concern, which you might not necessarily feel ready to do with a $100,000 1950s Patek Philippe "rare gold center seconds perpetual calendar wristwatch with moon phases," of which only 179 examples were produced, while you're outdoors barbecuing in the rain or changing a tire (though some people do— as F. Scott Fitzgerald said to Ernest Hemingway, "The rich are different from you and me.")

In short, whatever basic category you choose to collect in, there's still a lot to be said for a collection that represents some thought or instinct on your part and in which there is, if only to yourself, a recognizable coherence.

Money will obviously play a part. Some forms of collecting are ruinously expensive, some perfectly manageable. "Costly thy habit as thy purse can buy." At the beginning of building up a collection, it is sensible to start with modest steps rather than take big financial risks that leave you breathless and unable to enjoy what you've bought (or admit to anybody how much you spent). Later on, when your collection has taken on a certain *substance,* there may come along the object that you simply *have* to have to complete it, that star piece for which it is worth mortgaging the farm, but *don't* do it at the beginning, before you've really figured out what it is that you want to collect and in what direction you want the collection to go.

But to start with, you should ask yourself a basic question: Are you going to collect *antique* watches—that is, pocket watches, in all their varied forms—or modern wristwatches? To answer that question, you have to consider the subject of "complications."

Complications

*C*OMPLICATIONS ARE things we normally avoid in life, but in watches "complications" are considered highly desirable. Each complication adds to the value of a watch and, indeed, to the pleasure of owning it.

A typical (minor) complication, for example, found now even on many inexpensive watches, is a little window on the dial that shows the date. One largish step up from this would be additional windows for the month and the day of the week. To all this might be added the desirable and very attractive complication of a window showing the phase of the moon.

The big step up is taken when many major complications are linked mechanically in what are called *grandes complications,* one of which is the perpetual calendar, in which the mechanism not only automatically keeps track of the length of the month, but adjusts itself, every four years, to take into account the leap year. In short, provided the watch is set right to begin with and kept wound, it will show the correct date, day of the week, month, phase of the moon, and year for up to 100 years. The only human intervention necessary is to keep the watch wound, and if it has an automatic movement, even this necessity can be taken out of the owner's hands by placing the watch in a winding box, in which the watch is constantly rotated at a gentle speed to keep it fully wound when it isn't on the wrist.

Perpetual calendar watches have been around since the eighteenth century (Breguet constructed many of them before, during, and after the French Revolution, some of them using the revolutionary calendar), so there's no great

A Patek Philippe perpetual calendar pocket watch, manufactured in 1940,
with moon phases and leap-year indicator.
(Courtesy of Phillips, de Pury & Luxembourg)

trick to designing one—the trick is to miniaturize it so that it can be placed inside the small case of a modern wristwatch and to manufacture it at a price that is less than a king's ransom—and of course to make it run faultlessly.

Other complications include such features as a chronograph (or, to use the vernacular, a "stopwatch") which measures elapsed time, or the even more desirable "split-second chronograph," or *chronographe rattrapante*, with which two or more separate events can be timed simultaneously (as in recording the times of the first and second horses in a horse race); minute repetition, in which depressing a button on the watch activates a series of tiny gongs that sound out the exact time with a different chime for the hour, the quarter of an hour, and the minutes; and a power reserve indicator, usually a small dial that indicates how many hours the watch will run before it needs to be wound again.

Naturally, the more features combined in one watch, the rarer and more expensive it will be. Watches that are minute repeaters with a split-second chronograph, a perpetual calendar, and a power reserve indicator represent the elite in pocket watches and still today mark the more complicated and expensive wristwatches. Building all this into a pocket watch was a challenge, but building it into the tiny case of a wristwatch is something like a miracle. Bear in mind, we are not talking about electronic, digital, quartz, or battery-powered watches here—all these complications are *mechanical,* involving many delicately balanced, perfectly finished, microscopic wheels, gears, levers, and springs, placed in a watch that also has to include the normal time-keeping mechanism and, if it's automatic, the rotor and mechanism for automatically winding the mainspring.

Watchmakers make something of a fetish of complicated watches. To mark the year 2000, for example, Patek built the "Star Calibre 2000," a pocket watch with 1,118 handmade parts that included the following twenty-one functions, in addition to the basic one of telling the owner what time it is:

Running equation of time
Time of sunrise
Time of sunset
Twenty-four hour day/night display with passage of
    the sun
Perpetual calendar
Date
Leap-year cycle
Day of the week
Month
Season
Sky chart
Lunar orbit
Moon phases
Power reserve indicator
Power reserve indicator for the chime
Bidirectional winding
Precision adjustment of the movement from the
    outside
Pendant push button for opening spring-loaded covers
Westminster chime on five gongs
Minute repetition on five gongs
Chime-in-passing blocked when the mainspring is
    run down

It is difficult to imagine anybody having a use for a watch like this, but that is not really the point. The object is to prove that Patek can still design and manufacture a horological masterpiece, available to the (well-heeled) customer in yellow gold, rose gold, white gold, or platinum. To celebrate the 150th anniversary of the founding of Patek Philippe, the company produced the even more astonishing "Calibre 89" (1,728 hand-made parts), which had a total of thirty-three complications, the previous record having been twenty-four complications in the watch made for the distinguished American collector Henry J. Graves Jr. and sold to him in 1933.

In the view of purists, complications that are not integrated with the movement of a watch do not count. Thus, although certain makers have added to their watches things such as an altimeter or a hygrometer or a thermometer, these have no more place in a watch than would a bottle opener or a hoof pick, because they are not powered by the mainspring and integrated with the mechanism.

Note also that it would take most of us a great deal of time to figure out what to do with "Running equation of time," for instance, or "Lunar orbit," even if we knew what these meant (they're probably of practical interest only to astronomers). Photographs of Graves, a man of bottomless wealth allied to a passion for timekeeping, reveal a certain steely madness in the eyes on an otherwise ordinary face, which must have been necessary for him to plunge into the most recondite and complicated ways of measuring time and to demand of his many timepieces nothing less than absolute perfection.

The business of the chimes is still with us, the object being for the watch to mark the hour, the half hour, and the quarter hour not just by a chime, but with a carillon, like the signature tune of Big Ben, the famous clock in the tower over the House of Parliament in London. This is expensive and difficult to do in a pocket watch and even more so in a wrist-watch, and it therefore represents a valuable and exceedingly rare complication. It usually comes with a button to silence the carillon chimes so that you don't bother fellow dinner guests or other people at the theater.

Watches like these are the supreme aristocrats of watch-making, and seldom come up for sale. Patek published a whole book on their Star Calibre 2000 watch, and the book itself became a valued collector's item, which gives you some idea of the rarity of this kind of superwatch.

Nor is Patek alone in striving to produce these master-pieces of timekeeping. Audemars Piguet, always an innovator in the manufacture of complicated watches in the nineteenth century, makes a self-winding, water-resistant contemporary wristwatch with a perpetual calendar, and so does Blancpain, which adds to the perpetual calendar a split-second chrono-graph. The International Watch Company (IWC), a Swiss company that was famous in the late nineteenth century and early twentieth century for its superior pocket watches (Winston Churchill always wore an IWC pocket watch), reemerged as a high-tech watchmaker after World War II, one of its achievements being the "Da Vinci" wristwatch, which combines a chronograph and a perpetual calendar with moon phases in one relatively small water-resistant automatic watch. Indeed, for those who want the summit of timekeeping in a wristwatch, IWC offers its Il Destriero Scafusia "Oriental" model, which contains more than 750 hand-finished parts and has twenty-two complex functions, including a split-second chronograph, with minute and hour registers, perpetual calendar and moon phases, a unique four-digit display window for the year, and minute repetition; the whole movement is regulated by a tiny "tourbillon" mechanism that itself contains almost 100 tiny parts and weighs only 0.296 grams!

You will need good eyesight (or a strong pair of reading glasses) to make out the many tiny numbers, windows, dials, and hands on the face of a wristwatch that is only forty-two millimeters in diameter, but the point is that they're there. For the physician with a lot of money and good eyesight, Vacheron & Constantin makes a platinum medical "skeleton" watch, in which the entire movement is visible and hand engraved, and which includes a chronograph with minute register, arranged as a "pulsometer" for measuring the patient's heart rate. Going further up the scale of value, there is in fact hardly any major watchmaker who does not produce a variety of *montres de grandes complications* today,(such a watch must include a perpetual calendar, a split-second chronograph, and minute repetition), and it goes without saying that they represent an interesting (though expensive) area in which to collect. The most complicated wristwatch in the world, by Gerald Genta, which appears on the next page, is an example of just how far a watchmaker can go!

If what interests you are complications per se, then it may be worth considering collecting mid- to late-nineteenth-century pocket watches instead of wristwatches. They can be found with almost every imaginable complication, are made by any number of makers in Switzerland, Germany, France, and England, and go for prices mostly well below those of similarly complicated wristwatches, in part because to put

Gerald Genta—unique and most complicated wristwatch in the world. Self-winding double-train, water-resistant, with Westminster chime, Grande et Petite Sonnerie *and silent display, four gongs and four hammers, minute-repeating, perpetual calendar, leap-year indication, a second 24-hour time zone, 48-hour power reserve indicator for the gong and striking trains, with one-minute tourbillon regulator.*
(Photo by Antiquorum)

these complications into the small volume of a wristwatch case requires a miracle of miniaturization and in part because most people in contemporary society find it easier to wear a wristwatch than a pocket watch.

This sartorial problem can be alleviated (for men), as I have long since discovered, by wearing a waistcoat. The small pockets on the front of a waistcoat, in fact, were made for containing a watch, and a waistcoat looks better with a watch chain draped across the front of it. Placed snugly in the waistcoat pocket, the watch is secure, easy to reach, and well protected against theft, knocks, and the elements. Some people like to wear a pocket watch in the breast pocket of their jacket, with a chain linked into the button hole of the left lapel, which is a perfectly good solution until they take their jacket off, at which point they no longer have ready access to their watch. A pocket watch can be carried in your trouser pocket, with a chain fastened to a belt loop or to the belt itself or to the button on the trouser band for suspenders; this is certainly a neat solution for the summer, when you very likely won't be wearing a waistcoat and will often be walking around in shirtsleeves, but has the disadvantage that if you hit your side against a desk or a filing cabinet, you may damage the watch.

I collect pocket watches exclusively, so I have tried all these ways, and many more, of carrying (and securing) one, but the ideal solution remains a waistcoat, with an extra button hole cut vertically so that the chain can be looped through it and a cloth tab in each of the pockets, so that the chain can be fastened safely at the end that isn't connected to a watch. Older tailors know how to do all this, because these modifications were common for three-piece suits in the age of transition from the pocket watch to the wristwatch.[†] Some people like to have the watch pocket lined in suede leather, but suede tends to gather dirt and grit and leave scratches on the watch (exactly what it's supposed to prevent); a better solution is to have a small leather pouch for each of your pocket watches, to protect the finish. These pouches can often be found in every imaginable color and size at most watch shows or can be made by a leather specialist.

† Herzfeld, on Madison Avenue, makes my waistcoats and knows exactly how to add all the details that make wearing a pocket watch easy.

Because the value of a watch is radically affected by the number of complications it embodies, a brief discussion of these complications may be in order, bearing in mind that no two people are likely to agree on which are the most desirable.

In pocket watches, there's the essential difference between "open face" watches and "hunters," the latter having a spring-latched cover that closes over the face of the watch to protect the glass from impact. The hunter, as the word implies, was originally designed for fox hunters, who risked shattering the glass crystal over the face of their watch at every jump (or fall), and it gradually became a desirable form of case for active people. Hunters normally have the bow and winding crown at three o'clock rather than at twelve o'clock, the hinge of the cover at nine o'clock, and the cover is normally opened by pushing down on a small button set in the crown. Some people find hunters more interesting (and collectible) than open face watches, and because they are rarer, they are usually more expensive—that is to say, there will normally be a premium over the same grade and type of watch if the case is in the hunter format. Ultimately, however, it's a matter of taste. Some people like the whole business of drawing out the watch, opening the cover, looking at the time, then carefully, with the button depressed, lowering and relatching the cover and replacing the watch in the pocket (this is the correct way to close a hunter, rather than pushing the cover against the latch until it clicks, which will sooner or later result in wear and tear that will be difficult and expensive to repair). It makes looking at the time a kind of small, formal ceremony, full of seriousness, which Victorians understood well.

Bearing in mind, therefore, that pocket watches are divided into two different styles, the following small differences are likely to affect the rarity and the price of any watch.

A watch with a chronograph is always more desirable than a simple watch. A split-second chronograph is still more desirable by a very considerable margin. A minute register (that counts the minutes elapsed) is very desirable, and minute *and* hour registers more desirable still. On pocket watches, a small slide on the side of the case that locks the stopwatch, and thus prevents the owner from stopping or setting it in motion accidentally, is very desirable, and on wristwatches a single button operating through the crown is vastly rarer and more desirable than the usual two round, square, or oval buttons above and below the crown.

Numerous small differences in design tend to make a calendar complication more desirable if present. In general, the more modern calendar watches will have small rectangular apertures for the date, day of the week, and month. Older watches will have small dials, which are certainly more attractive, but harder to read. The portrait of the moon as it appears to mark the phases of the moon can vary from modern and simple to wonderfully detailed and interesting in older watches—this is a matter of taste, really. Perpetual calendar watches often have a dial that registers the current year within a four-year cycle, because they have to compensate for the leap year. Most such watches have small indented push buttons in the case to adjust all these functions should you forget to wind the watch. Modern wristwatches of the more expensive kind usually come with a special device to press these buttons down without scratching the case; for those that don't (and that includes all pocket watches), a large supply of wooden tooth picks is recommended.

A few further small differences. To indicate the date, some watches have a "flying" date hand instead of a dial or a rectangular aperture. Usually, this complication consists of a half circle, with the dates, from 1 through 31 on its circumference. The hand moves one day at a time until it reaches the last day in the month, then it "flies" back to 1. This is generally thought to be a more elegant and complicated system for recording the date than the other systems and will add to the value of the watch,

Power reserve indicators are valued in both wristwatches and pocket watches. The most elegant in form is probably that of the Breguet watches, in which this function is gracefully integrated in the design of the dial, but it is always a desirable complication.

On military wristwatches (and others), a mechanism that allows the wearer to synchronize the watch exactly is highly valued. There are various ways to accomplish this, the simplest being that the sweep seconds hand of the watch can be stopped at "twelve" by pulling out the crown; other watches have a separate button to accomplish this, but it is always a desirable feature. In older watches, the sweep seconds hand itself is comparatively rare—most of them have a small dial to mark the seconds at six o'clock—and may add value to the watch.

A very rare, but mechanically interesting complication is the full "two-train" movement that features bidirectional winding. In minute-repeating pocket watches, this means that there are two separate sources of power, one to run the watch, the other to operate the gongs for the repetition. In such watches, the crown is usually wound in the conventional direction (clockwise) to wind the movement and in the opposite direction (counter-clockwise) to wind the repeating mechanism. Two-train watches in which the repeater mechanism is operated by a button in the crown are often far more valuable than an ordinary repeater with a slide on the side of the case to operate the mechanism.

"World Time" watches are another special category. The system usually seen now was designed by the famous Swiss watchmaker Louis Cottier (1894–1966), and the best of them still use his unique system for world timekeeping, which includes an annular ring around the dial with the names of thirty or so of the world's cities engraved on it. You set the ring for the city where you currently are and then read off the time in other cities. Another ring is usually divided into two halves, one shaded, one not, to show whether it is daytime or nighttime in a city. This system, originally developed for pocket watches, was also adapted to wristwatches, and some of these watches—those made by Patek specifically—are regularly among the more expensive watches at auctions, because they are comparatively rare. The patent on the system has long since expired, so cheaper imitations are to be found in abundance now.

Other systems include watches that have two separate hour hands, permitting the watch to show two different times (for example, the time where you are now, and the time at home, if you're traveling) or to show Greenwich Mean Time and local time. There are numerous other solutions to the time zone problem, though the one with the two hour hands seems to me the simplest and the most elegant, and these watches will always command a premium.

Then there are watches ingeniously designed for the apparent purpose of making it difficult to read the time.

They include "regulator" watches, in which the conventional minute hand goes around normally, but a small hand set in a subsidiary dial indicates the hour; "epicycloidal" wrist-watches, with a half circle for the seconds and a "floating" hour on a revolving transparent disk to indicate the hour; "jumping hour" wristwatches and pocket watches in which the seconds hand goes around normally, but the hour "jumps" into view as it changes in a small rectangular aperture at the top of the dial; and many variations on watches that show the hour and the seconds in small apertures. It is much more difficult to tell time by these watches than by a normal watch dial, to which our eyes have become accustomed, but they would, of course, constitute an interesting and unusual variation for a collection.

There is, of course, more and *much* more. The watch industry has always specialized in mechanical ingenuity, so mechanics is an area in which a sound knowledge of watch design and watchmaking are absolutely necessary if you're going to start collecting with complications in mind. Explanations of the various complications and types of movement are not easy to come by (though the guides put out by Roy Ehrhardt at the Heart of America Press in Umatilla, Florida, come as close as any I have read to explaining all this in simple terms), but the time to start thinking about exactly what an "anchor chronometer" is shouldn't be when you're bidding on one at an auction.

Generally speaking, the better auction catalogs—those from Christie's, Sotheby, Antiquorum, and Phillips —describe most of these functions very well, certainly well enough to give you a good grounding in the world of watch complications (and their relative value).

The main thing to keep in mind is that the watch, whether it is a pocket watch or a wristwatch, has to present an attractive and visually harmonious appearance, however complicated the movement may be. If the dial is crowded, impossible to read, and unattractive, the watch is unlikely to please you over the long run. This is a question of individual taste, of course, but it is one to which you should pay some attention before you add a watch to your collection.

Naturally, you need to consider all the usual warnings even with a watch that can do everything except fly: Who is the manufacturer? What kind of condition is it in (complicated watches are agonizingly difficult to overhaul or repair, and few watchmakers are qualified to work on them)? What is its history? What have similar watches sold for in recent sales?

One thing is certain—watches with complications, other things being equal, are always likely to be of interest and very likely to climb in value; the rarer the complications, the better. Repeaters are highly valued by most collectors; chronographs (particularly split-second chronographs with one or two registers) are not only useful for timing sporting events, but likely to gain in value over the years; and perpetual calendar watches represent a whole subsegment of collecting, because plenty of people out there are interested *only* in perpetual calendars and collect nothing else. Watches that combine all these functions—*les montres de grandes complications*—are, of course, the élite of them all.

Complications offer the opportunity for an interesting and very special form of collecting. My friend Edward Faber, a New York City dealer who specializes in vintage watches, has very often suggested that it makes sense to collect a single brand or make of watch and to buy the best ones you can find and afford, then trade them off from time to time to acquire one with some interesting additional complication until eventually, you have a collection of *montres de grandes complications* by one maker. Naturally, this process takes self-discipline, some knowledge, and the ability to move fast when that rare and complicated watch comes along. Another possibility is to collect watches with important complications by different makers—say, perpetual calendar wristwatches, starting with the less extravagant ones and building up eventually to the rarer and more expensive ones by the great makers. In short, you must have an end in sight, a *goal* for the collection, an area of interest and knowledge, rather than collect randomly.

In any event, the quickest way to learn about the *inside* of a watch is to start learning about complications; that's important because to collect watches sensibly (and with any hope of profit) you have to have at least *some* informed and educated interest in what's inside that shiny case and under that gleaming, neatly numbered dial—to have some idea, to put it bluntly, of "what makes it tick."

5

The Aesthetics of Time

HERE ARE two different aesthetic views of time. The first derives from the mathematics of time itself—the way in which human beings, over the centuries, have broken down and divided time into segments that represent, in effect, a miniature version of the cosmos itself. Just as the whole universe consists of bodies revolving around each other in fixed orbits at approximately fixed rates, the structure of even the most complex watch is built in the form of circles revolving around circles (geared drives of various kinds moving geared wheels, which in turn drive other wheels at various rates) to transform the passage of time into precise fragments called seconds, minutes, and hours.

The mathematics of time, therefore, mirrors the structure of the universe, but, in an engineering sense, so does the design and structure of any timepiece. Carrying a mechanical watch, however humble, is tantamount to carrying a miniature of the cosmos in your pocket or on your wrist. Human beings have different ways in which they record distances (miles and kilometers, for example), different ways in which they record weight (metric tons, U.S. tons, British tonnes), different ways in which they measure liquid volume (liters, pints), but in every culture the second, the minute, and the hour are the same length. During the French Revolution, extremists, in addition to renaming the months, attempted to impose a decimal calendar and decimal measurement of time, as well as a metric circle of 400 degrees, but unlike the metric measurement of distance, weight, and volume, it never caught on: time is divided by twelve, reflecting the 360 degrees of a circle, and every watch is therefore a replication of the solar system.

Made in 1790 in Paris by Blanc Laine, this unusual pocket watch shows both the normal 24-hour dial and the then-new, revolutionary (and politically correct) decimal 10-hour timekeeping system.
(Photo by Antiquorum)

The aesthetics of timekeeping and watchmaking are mathematical, and a look at the working drawings of distinguished innovators in the field of time measurement is highly recommended, even for the amateur collector. To look at the drawings of Abraham-Louis Breguet, for example, is to be astonished by his sheer power of invention and by his total command of applied mathematics and geometry. Before the French Revolution, he had already designed and built an efficient self-winding watch, for example, and many of his watches include complications that are rare even today.

To appreciate just what marvelous instruments watches are—for we have come to take them for granted over the past 150 years—it is important to make some effort to understand how they work, to take note of the meticulous and painstaking attention to detail, the mathematical accuracy, as well as the sophisticated engineering that even the cheapest of mechanical watches embodies. That is not to say that you should necessarily take a penknife to your watch or to one you are thinking of buying and pry open the back, or take up watchmaking as a hobby, but some knowledge of the various kinds of movements and their refinements will help you to understand why one watch is valuable, whereas another, to all appearances very similar, is far less so.

Once again, the catalogs of the major auction houses are very helpful in this respect, because most of them describe the movement of each watch in considerable detail—Antiquorum catalogs give the most detail and sometimes contain useful little essays on various unusual features in a movement and why they are important or significant in the history of watchmaking.

Collecting watches without any knowledge of "what

makes them tick" is like collecting guns without knowing the difference between a matchlock, a flintlock, and a percussion weapon, or like collecting cars without any knowledge of what's under the hood. That is not to say that it's impossible to do—plenty of collectors are interested only in appearance and price—but one of the pleasures of collecting watches lies in learning to understand and appreciate exactly how they work and what makes them different and special.

Certainly, if you're going to *buy* them, it would be a good idea to develop at least a rough idea of what descriptions mean. For example, "Calibre 1868 hand-engraved, gilt brass and rhodium-plated, 76 jewels, lateral lever escapement with titanium escapement bridge, flying one-minute tourbillon regulator with titanium cage and 3 equidistant arms, monometallic balance adjusted for heat, cold and 6 positions, shock absorber, self-compensating Breguet balance-spring, repeating on gongs by activating slide on the band." (See the glossary for the explanation of these terms.)

This, as it happens, is a description of the movement for an IWC minute-repeater, astronomic, chronograph wristwatch, and some idea of the complexity of the IWC movement can be gauged by the fact that a Rolex "Daytona" wrist chronograph in the same catalog has a movement with fifteen jewels.

A working knowledge of the principal features of watch movements is probably a good idea if, as in this case, you are going to contemplate paying up to a quarter of a million dollars for one. You may as well know what you're paying for!

On the other hand, as I've mentioned, aesthetics matter. Many people are more interested in what a watch *looks* like than in what it contains; this has always been true and explains why, except in Switzerland and in certain shops such as Tourneau or Wempe in New York City, watches have been sold by jewelers, almost from the beginning of the trade, and still are today. Watches are—or are *meant* to be—decorative as well as useful and in general are thought to make some sort of statement about the owner's taste, wealth, and social importance, much as jewelry does for women, so it is hardly surprising that a great many collectors are more interested in appearance than in monometallic balances.

Just at the moment, for instance, enameled pocket watches, though out of fashion for decades—indeed, since the mid-nineteenth century—are suddenly beginning to interest collectors again, and new ones are even being made. The art of enameling a painting or a portrait on the back of a pocket watch or on the dial of a wristwatch is difficult to do and therefore expensive. Such watches were popular in the seventeenth and eighteenth centuries, but by the Victorian era men mostly preferred the solid assurance of gold, and enameled watches were for the most part either made for ladies, in small sizes meant to be pinned by a ribbon to the dress, or in elaborate and highly colored form for the Chinese, Turkish, and Indian markets. Nevertheless, enameled watches continued to be made, either in the form of semitransparent enamel over engine-turned or engraved gold (known as *guilloche*) or in the form of paintings and portraits enameled on the outside or—more discreetly—on the inside of the case back. Hunting scenes and maritime scenes were popular, as were patriotic scenes—Napoleon crossing the Alps for the French market, or Napoleon retreating from Moscow for the Russian market. Wives gave their husband a gold watch with an enameled portrait of themselves inside

*"Farewell to the Beloved"—a beautifully enameled pocket watch,
mounted with pearls, ca. 1830, made for the Chinese market.*
(Photo by Antiquorum)

the case for significant birthdays; monarchs gave out watches
with their portrait or their royal coat of arms enameled on
the outside of the back cover; for men with that kind of
sense of humor, a watch might have a peaceful landscape
enameled on the outside of the back cover and an erotic
scene on the inside.

Up until a few years ago, it would have been possible to
assemble an interesting collection of enameled watches without spending a fortune, but now prices have skyrocketed for
the really good ones. Despite that, there are still a lot of enameled watches out there, and somebody with a discerning eye
could probably put together a pretty interesting collection.

If you find that you like, say, 1920s wristwatches, then
go for it. If what interests you is collecting early Rolexes
(you'd be starting a little late, but there are still many of them
around), then learn as much as you can about them (read, for
example, *Collecting Rolex Wristwatches,* by Osvaldo Patrizzi, or
Rolex: An Unauthorized History, by Dowling and Hess), and

buy the ones that appeal to you. The main thing, in my opinion, is to collect those things that make you happy to wear and to look at and that appeal strongly to your own aesthetic sense, and then not to get derailed from that objective.

There is nothing wrong in collecting watches because of their looks, if only because people have always bought watches at least in part on their looks. A case in point is the Jaeger-LeCoultre Reverso wristwatch, with a rectangular case in which the watch itself can be swiveled so that either the dial or the back of the watch is face up. This was an early and ingenious attempt to solve one of the undeniable problems of the wristwatch—the ease with which it is possible to smash the crystal when playing violent sports (polo, rugby), or when fighting in a war. A simple flip protects the dial of the Reverso watch—only the solid back of the case (which can be engraved with initials or something else) is exposed on the wrist. The Reverso was very popular among the sporting set in the 1920s and 1930s, but then began to seem old-fashioned once Rolex started to produce the waterproof Oyster case, with its tough, synthetic crystal, and advertised its rugged qualities by having it worn by cross-Channel swimmers or by fastening it to the hull of a deep-sea-diving bathysphere and carried to fantastic depths. The Reverso came back into popularity in the 1960s and 1970s, this time not for its sporting qualities, but for its looks; it gradually came to be made with increasingly complicated movements, as opposed to the simple, rugged movement of the original, and is now something of a fashion statement. It's one of those things that either you like or you don't—I've known people who would never wear any other kind of watch and people who couldn't see the point of them at all—but that lends itself to collecting, because it has a huge variety of dials (almost as varied as those of early Rolexes, no two of which seem to be exactly the same), and now, of course, a certain variety of movements too. A collection of these Reversos might be very interesting—*if,* of course, you like the look of the watch.

Pre-World War II American wristwatches, by Gruen or Hamilton Watch Co. or Bulova (among others), can be fascinating, with a huge variety of cases and dials, from the severe and conventional to the brilliantly unusual art deco. In the 1920s and 1930s, American watches were often much more interesting in design and a good deal more varied than Swiss ones. Once again, this is no longer a cheap area in which to collect, but as compared to collecting vintage Patek Philippe watches or nineteenth century *montres de grandes complications,* it's still pretty reasonable, and there are an awful lot of American watches still out there to collect. Many American manufacturers produced watches in the millions before going out of business.

The mid- to late-nineteenth century American railroad pocket watches are often extraordinarily designed, with boldly legible and often strikingly attractive dials. Many of these watches have unique systems that prevent the owner of the watch from accidentally changing the time while winding it. This feature was developed after a series of catastrophic railway collisions in which it turned out that the conductor was at fault through having pulled the crown of his watch out only part way to wind it and thus moved the hands instead. These watches were therefore equipped with a safety device to prevent that from happening, and the watchmakers also took the precaution of designing dials that were impossible to misread—another cause of accidents. The result is that the American railroad pocket watch is uniquely special and interesting to collect. None of these watches could possibly be mistaken for a Swiss watch of the same period; they're actually early examples of what later came to be called "industrial design" and by the standards of the day are remarkably sturdy, reliable, and, in some cases, very handsome indeed. Most of them are in silver or nickel or gold fill—they were working tools for workingmen, after all—though many exist in solid gold, made as engraved presentation pieces for retiring railway presidents and senior executives. Unquestionably, this is an area in which it would be possible, even today, to build up an interesting collection without having to bid up in the stratosphere, where the Henry Graves *grandes complications* pocket watch, for example, went for over $11 million on auction or a Patek Philippe rectangular platinum calendar wristwatch fetched more than $1 million. For a comparatively modest amount of money, it would be possible to build up a stunning collection of significant American railroad watches and probably not impossible to find out a good deal about the original owners and which railroad they worked for. Well, it's a thought.

Judging from a recent auction catalog, that thought has occurred to other people. And not surprisingly, *scores* of successful American watch manufacturers produced watches of unique and ingenious design in vast numbers, no two of which, despite sophisticated mass-production techniques, seem to look exactly alike.

The same could be said for "deck watches," large pocket watches that are usually made with a silver case and stored in a wooden box like a miniature marine chronometer—which is exactly what they were, in fact. In the naval and maritime world, officers used deck watches, regularly checked against the ship's main chronometer on the bridge, to work out navigational problems and to ensure that the whole ship ran on the correct time. Deck watches were often kept on the bridge in a wooden box with a glass cover, one on the port side and one on the starboard, as auxiliaries to the larger ship's chronometer, which was usually placed amidships, close to the compass binnacle.

These deck watches were still being manufactured throughout World War II, and the ones made in the United States, Switzerland, and France for the U.S. Navy are extremely interesting and comprise a whole range of varied, rugged instruments, well worth collecting. Royal Navy deck watches are usually of British manufacture and are marked on the dial with the broad arrow that identifies all British military stores. German naval deck watches are usually outsize silver pocket watches from among the best of German and British watchmakers, of chronometer quality, with very legible dials, and of course are stamped with a contract number and the Reichsmarine symbol or, from 1933 to 1945, with the Reichsmarine eagle and swastika. Quite a few of these deck watches are around, and if you don't mind the size—they're bigger than normal pocket watches—and the fact that they need polishing (not a problem on a naval vessel, of course, where most of the crew's day is spent polishing things anyway), they would make the basis for an interesting, handsome, and very unusual collection.

Once again, I am not suggesting that you should necessarily rush out and follow my advice, but merely that if you carve out a *defined area* that interests you and collect the best examples you can find—and that also appeal to you aesthetically—you will be laying the base for a collection that will give you great pleasure, and over the years may be of unique interest and value as you learn more about it. I myself, for example, have very little interest in Breitling aviator watches—in part because they have so many tiny numbers on the dial that I can't read them, even when I'm sitting at home with the desk light on, let alone sitting in a pilot's seat in the dark flying an aircraft—but some people love these watches, and the sheer complexity of the dials is fascinating. The Breitling Navitimer QP, for instance, has nine different functions on the dial, ten separate "hands," and, according to one catalog, it provides "a perpetual calendar, the 52 weeks, a round button chronograph with two registers, a tachometer and a logarithmic sliding-rule," which will give you plenty to study if you have a mathematical mind and good eyesight. Other Breitlings are almost as complex and specialized, and they are not, by Patek or "collectible Rolex" standards, all that expensive.

This kind of complicated wristwatch, if it appeals to you, can form the basis of a good collection—the Longines "Lindbergh" aviator watches, for instance, designed by Lindbergh himself and first marketed in 1932, are extremely interesting (with an oversize crown so that the pilot can wind it or reset it without having to remove his gloves), and although you may not need such complexities as the "hour angle," it's intriguing to see the amount of navigational information that a wristwatch could be designed to carry.

Once you pick a specific look or style of watch, the rest is easy—keep your eyes open, cruise the Net, and follow the auctions. You can pick old or new; it's really up to you. I'm not myself really enamored by the look of ultramodern watches, but if you are, you can collect, say, Daniel Roth designs or the even more futuristic Alain Silberstein watches, with their strange-looking hands and acidic bright colors. Why not? It's your collection.

At its extreme level, this advice applies, for example, to collecting Swatch watches. When Nicholas Hayek took it upon himself to revive the Swiss watch industry, which was succumbing in the 1970s to competition from Japan at the lower end of the market, he deliberately chose to use a single, simple electronic module to power the watch—something that could be swiftly and cheaply mass-produced and assembled—but decided to clad it in an endless variety of cases and straps, chosen for their appeal to young people who wore a watch as a statement of fashion but didn't want to be tied to it for a lifetime or even until it looked out of date.

The Swatch was thus, from the beginning, not only a *disposable* watch—you could throw it away when you got bored with it—but one with a built-in potential as a collectible. It could be decorated with photographs of Marilyn Monroe or with Andy Warhol photographs or with any number of other themes, artwork, or designs and produced in "limited" editions. Artists vied with each other to design Swatch watches; collectors' groups were established all over the world; and the Swatch became a kind of design icon, the watch you bought for the way it looked, just like a pair of shoes. If you bought what you liked among the limited editions and put them away, lo and behold, before anybody had even thought much about it, not only was the humble Swatch being collected, but certain of the rarer designer editions were going for substantial amounts of money. Here, after all, was a watch where the inner workings were of no interest to anybody at all—they were all basically the same—so the interest and attention was on the looks.

Of course, it's a long way from collecting Swatch watches to collecting watches that have several *layers* of appeal—aesthetic, historical, and mechanical, for example—but there's nothing wrong in choosing to collect what appeals to your eye, and to some extent all collectors do so, even those whose primary interest lies in one high-end brand or in a particular kind of movement or combination of complications. At some level, even those collectors who don't know exactly what they're trying to collect will recognize it when they see it, rather like love at first sight, and say, "Yes, that's it, that's exactly what I've had in mind, right there!"

Watches, too, are a kind of love affair, or else why collect them? And, as in love affairs, although looks aren't the whole story, they're certainly part of it.

6

Who Me, Collect?

*B*EING A collector sounds like a serious thing to be, conjuring up an image of the connoisseur, magnifying glasses perched on his nose, surrounded by priceless objets d'art and courted by dealers and auctioneers, like a figure out of a Hogarth etching. Almost all of us, in fact, collect (or have collected) *something* and will continue to do so throughout our lives. Not all of these collections are valuable or important—indeed, most of them are decidedly not—but collecting appears to be a more or less universal human habit, shared in nature by jackdaws (among other birds), which, as everybody knows, like to collect shiny objects in their nests. Even people who led nomadic lives, such as the American Indian tribes of the West, and therefore had to be able to gather all their belongings up in a bundle, still burdened themselves with collections of tiny stones or scalps or sacred objects. A collection, whatever its nature, not only comforts and pleases, but *stabilizes,* pins the collector down in time and space, *anchors* him, so to speak, and provides a readily available source of order and purpose, even during moments when life is at its most meaningless and difficult.

Still, what *is* a collection? Most men have a lot of ties, but we would not regard them as "a collection," necessarily. Most women have several drawers full of lingerie, but we would hesitate to call that "a collection." In both cases, it would be possible to *have* "a collection": a collection of unusual or special ties, say, the wide, painted ties that were popular in the 1940s; collections of lingerie of course exist, but usually because they represent the secret treasure trove and fantasies of a male fetishist. In short, something special has to be added to a series of objects in order to make its owner "a collector."

The key to collecting is *desire,* the desire to possess certain specific objects that stimulate our interest, our fantasies, or our preconceptions about beauty. But desire alone is not enough; desire must be accompanied by a strong sense of personal choice, a reason to pick or value one object instead of another, an *informed* choice of period, style, and aesthetics, a certain structure and order.

The watch collector does not collect watches in order to know what the time is—he can get that from the radio, after all; he collects watches first of all because a certain type and style of watch seems to him beautiful and interesting and, second, because watches in general represent order and stability, the fixed and unalterable rate at which time passes. Here are instruments that, from their inception, have measured in precise segments the one unchangeable reality within which we live—the passage of time, always moving forward, never back, so that with each tiny, precise click of the seconds or minute hand there is just that much less time left to us. "Where did the time go?" we ask ourselves when we've had a good time. "How time flies," we say when we feel it's passing too quickly, before we can grab our fair share of it. We cannot possess time or stop it or hold onto it; it's like water running through our fingers. But we *can* possess the instruments that *measure* time—hence, the endless fascination with clocks and watches, and the fact that so many people collect them, often without quite knowing why, except for the fact that they're pretty or mechanically interesting or expensive, or simply because they draw envious glances from those who know the value of the object on our wrist.

Somebody who buys a second watch because he might need it when the first one is being repaired or gets broken isn't collecting—he's simply behaving prudently (or perhaps a little *over*prudently, like a man wearing a belt *and* suspenders to keep his trousers up). A man who buys a second watch because it in some way harmonizes with the first or because it seems interesting to be able to change watches—one, say, for everyday wear, the other for formal wear or for making a splash—has made the first step towards collecting.

It almost goes without saying that money as such has nothing to do with being a collector—most serious collectors can hardly even imagine selling the object they've just acquired, however big the profit might be. It is their intense interest in this particular object, or *type* of object, that fuels them, not the thought it might be a good investment.

Often, in fact, some of the more serious collectors can hardly ever hope to profit from their collection because it is simply too specialized. I am partial to late-nineteenth-century pocket watches with some kind of complication (which have a fixed value), but also accompanied by the maximum amount of documentation about the original owner—who he was, why he bought the watch, or under what circumstances it was presented to him—but however much all that paperwork means to me, I know how difficult it will be to find a buyer who feels the same thrill at the sight of a yellowed bill of sale or a file full of correspondence relating to the watch. Many collectors don't even want a watch that has been monogrammed or bears an inscription, whereas for me, these details are exactly the things that attract my attention and spark my curiosity in the first place. I like my watches to have a history or, failing that, a mystery. To each his own.

The first step to collecting is to give in to what you really like—if it is big, outsize watches, fine, or chronographs with all the bells and whistles, also fine. Don't try to think ahead to what the next purchaser may like at the point when you decide to sell your collection, concentrate instead on what *you* like in the here and now. Fortunately, the watch industry, from the very outset, has tried to please every possible taste and need; seldom has a relatively simply mechanical function—timekeeping—been delivered in so wide a variety of packages and at such astonishingly different levels of value.

That remains true even today—just go to a major watch store and look around at the bewildering and dazzling variety of what's available and at prices that range from the relatively low to the simply fabulous—and was perhaps even more true in the eighteenth and nineteenth centuries, when there was simply no limit to how far watchmakers and their customers would go to make a timepiece unique, valuable, and one of a kind: from a recent catalog I pick, more or less at random, a rare gold-and-enamel "singing bird" watch of 1815, for example, in which a small enameled and jeweled canary pops up out of the center of the watch to flap its wings and sing a song; or Breguet's famous *montres à tact* ("tactful watches"), small

A very rare 18kt gold and enamel pocket watch, ca. 1815, which contains a bird that pops up, sings, flaps its wings and opens its beak to mark the hour.
(Photo by Antiquorum)

Breguet watch à tact, sold on 10 Vendémiaire (2 October) 1802. Note arrow on back of case that allows the owner to feel what time it is without looking at the watch.
(Photo by Antiquorum)

masterpieces in which a moving bar, often in the shape of a jeweled arrow, on the back of the watch allowed the wearer to reach into his pocket and determine what time it was without seeming rude by having to take out the watch and look at it; or a watch with a dial on the front for the hours and minutes, and a separate dial on the back for the seconds (made by Pierre Le Roy in Paris in 1774); or a watch elaborately decorated with an American eagle and the Stars and Stripes in enamel and diamonds on the front of the case, and the Turkish Star and Crescent in diamonds on the back (no doubt an early diplomatic presentation piece).

Today, too, it is possible to buy a solid-gold Rolex with the bezel set in diamonds, or with a dial on which diamonds are used to mark the numerals, or even to have a dial covered with pavé diamonds; or you could purchase a Patek Philippe wristwatch in platinum, with diamonds instead of numerals. The urge to embellish, to turn the watch into a symbol of wealth and a dazzling piece of jewelry, is as strong now as it was in the days of Marie Antoinette and Louis XVI, when watches made for the court were expected to be priceless works of the jeweler's art—veritable eyestoppers—as well as mechanical marvels.

Watch ordered by Louis XVI, and started in 1789, this masterpiece by Louis Berthoud is a double-face quarter repeating Montre Marine *with independent equation of time of special design and annual calendar.*
(Photo by Antiquorum)

Nor is it just the *montres de grande luxe* that provided—and still provide—a diversity to appeal to every taste. "Masonic" watches—bearing on the dial and case a plethora of Masonic symbols and messages—were very popular throughout the mid- to late-nineteenth century and at the beginning of the twentieth century, and are seldom all that expensive today; indeed, many of them were only a cut above the so-called dollar watches of the period. Watches with sporting and hunting scenes on the dial or engraved (often in bas relief) on the case were hugely popular and often comparatively inexpensive, as were watches that commemorated horse races, beloved dogs, shooting festivals (always very popular in Switzerland, land of William Tell and the *Schutzfeste*), or watches given as prizes for sporting events, and so forth.

For years in the late nineteenth century, it was fashionable for men in evening dress to carry a pocket watch set inside a hollowed out gold coin—a $20 gold piece was a favorite because of its convenient size—and in the twentieth century a different version continued to be popular. In fact, Corum made something of a specialty of producing wristwatches with a real gold coin as a dial, which were very fashionable in the 1970s and 1980s, especially among successful Wall Street types. Today, they would not be difficult to collect—they still have a certain fascination (I mean, you keep looking at it and asking yourself, "How on earth did they *do* that?), and they were made with several different coins, a U.S. $20 gold piece, a very handsome Mexican gold coin, and perhaps others, too. Watches with nautical themes abound, from gold presentation watches and deck watches in the nineteenth century to modern wristwatches with tiny enameled pennants representing the correct signal flag numerals in place of the ordinary numbers. Drivers' watches were popular in the 1920s and 1930s, made with a rectangular dial, like a horizontal strip, with a raised, wedge-shaped crystal so you could see the time without, presumably, taking your hands off the wheel. In more recent years, the firm of Girard-Perregaux has made rather a specialty of chronograph wristwatches matched to some of the more exotic Ferrari models; one of the more exclusive series commemorates the "limited edition" Ferrari F50—the first 349 watches were available only to actual purchasers of the car and had the individual car's VIN number engraved on the back of the case, along with an enameled Ferrari crest; others have featured dials in Ferrari "Corso" red or in carbon fiber, the wildly expensive textured material used for the bodywork in Ferrari's latest race cars. Divers' watches come in an infinite variety of types, by no means limited to the more familiar Rolex models, for those who have an interest in SCUBA diving. Rolex itself has produced a number of special watches, including a much-coveted version of the familiar "Submariner" watch bearing the name of the Comex company on the dial and the rare "Milgauss" watch, which has an internal case back of iron to prevent magnetism from affecting the watch's accuracy. Divers' wristwatches, of course, have been produced for the navies of most major nations, including Italy and the former Soviet Union, and it would certainly be possible to build up a pretty comprehensive collection of them, even if you're only going to wear them in the bath.

Watchmaking, from the beginning, was never a one-size-fits-all business, and even with the advent of industrialization in the late nineteenth century, when the American watch industry was turning out millions of watches a year and watch companies were using the most up-to-date methods (for the day) of mass production, the manufacturers still sought to provide an infinity of different styles and faces to meet every taste. The cheap American watch became so popular and so widely admired for reliability, value, and sturdiness all over the world, that Swiss makers began stamping their own low-priced products with the names of American manufacturers (usually with one or two letters changed as a protection against lawsuits). Manufacturers recognized early on that although it paid to standardize the works of a watch, or at least as many parts and components as they could, the customer still wanted a choice in terms of the dial and the case—in other words, the watch, however cheap, was still a piece of jewelry. Henry Ford's remark that the customer could have a Ford in any color he wanted provided it was black was in that sense the antithesis of the watch industry's experience: the watch customer might get pretty much the same movement in a watch wherever he bought it, at any rate below a certain price level, but he could have it in any style he wanted and for a little more could even have it gold or silver plated. If he was a Mason or a member of the Benevolent Protective Order of Elks or a Rotarian, local jewelry stores would certainly have a choice of such watches in stock. These watches—and those for unimaginably more clubs, associations, and orders—can be found in any pawn shop, secondhand store, or watch and jewelry show, and they might form the basis of an interesting collection, rich in American historical associations.

At a higher level, but not unconnected to watches made for club members, are watches presented to valued employees, supporters, or clients. They are likely to be rather more expensive than the watches people would ordinarily buy for themselves, ranging from the better grades of American watches to the most expensive Swiss watches. Many retirement watches are handsome pieces, indeed, and offer a unique opportunity for some research into the life of the recipient and the history of the firm or company for which he worked. Some of the European ones are amazing pieces, especially those made for kings or queens to present to people of importance.

Patek Philippe perpetual calendar watch with moon phases, bearing on the back of the case the coat of arms of King Vittorio Emanuele of Italy, manufactured in 1867—a typical royal presentation piece.
(Photo courtesy of Phillips, de Pury & Luxembourg)

Monarchs, in those days, traveled with a trunk full of presents for handing out en route, with an equerry in charge of the trunk to make sure recipients got the proper present for their station in life. A tie pin for the hotel concierge, monogrammed cuff links for the hotel manager, monogrammed cigarette cases for people of a certain importance, diamond pins and brooches with the royal crest for willing ladies, elaborate monogrammed gold watches for their husbands or for men of the highest importance. The less significant the monarch was, the more elaborate and widespread the gift giving would be—Queen Victoria, the kaiser, the Austro-Hungarian emperor, and the czar could afford to be less than lavish in handing out trinkets, whereas the kings of Serbia or Romania or the king of Egypt felt obliged to make up for the relative lack of importance of their respective countries in the Balance of Power. That explains why so many of these royal presentation pieces—the watches especially—are marked with the portrait, the royal crest, and the monogram of comparatively insignificant monarchs, whereas one from Queen Victoria or Edward VII would be a rare and major find. Probably the last monarchs to give out lavish and expensive luxury watches on a big scale are the late King Farouk of Egypt, who seems to have kept Vacheron & Constantin busy for years making watches with his portrait and monogram, and the Saudi kings, who continue to hand out Patek Philippe wristwatches and pocket watches with their portraits painted on the dial. Judging by the number of the latter that show up in auction catalogs, many of the recipients must sell their watch almost as soon as they receive it. Farouk's presentation watches, on the other hand, are very often beautiful pocket watches, with significant complications, reflecting the fact that Farouk, whatever his faults as a monarch, was himself an impassioned collector of watches.

A collection of royal presentation watches would be a nice ambition, though I have yet to see one. This is yet another of those ambiguous areas of collecting in which some people find such watches interesting (and potentially valuable), whereas others attach no value to the fact that a watch was presented to somebody by a monarch. The Saudi presentation watches, for example, sometimes go for *less* than the same Patek would sell for *without* the portrait of the Saudi king on the dial, either because there are simply too many of them around or because collectors don't particularly value the Saudi royal family.

Keep all this firmly in mind when you set out to build up a collection. When people tell you that watches retain their value—or increase their value—better than stocks, it is worth reminding yourself that this rule probably applies only to the very upper crust of watch collecting—the new or "as new" luxury wristwatches of the great makers, with significant complications, and to genuinely important vintage watches of museum quality. A collection that interests (and pleases) you is not necessarily going to interest or please somebody else, and the more exotic, esoteric, or special your interests are, the more pronounced this difference is likely to be.

For this reason, it's important to know whether you are collecting for pleasure (and possible long-term gain) or for short-term gain or simply gathering what you like under one roof or in one drawer. Those who collect for pleasure ought not to assume (and generally don't) that their collection will necessarily soar in value, and they recognize that any increase is likely to take place over the long haul. Those who collect oddities—wristwatches with rectangular cases designed to resemble a Rolls Royce grill, for example (or wristwatches with a portrait of King Ib'n Saud on the dial)—may find, if they decide to sell one day, that it takes a long time before a buyer with similar tastes turns up, cash in hand. (Of course, the alternative "small world" principle of collection must also be taken into account, which decrees that if you collect something *truly* bizarre and special, you're likely to know most of the other people who share your passion, because there aren't going to be many of them, so at the first hint that you're thinking of selling, they'll come running to buy.) Those who collect for short-term gain—which is, in essence, speculating—need a nose for the marketplace and for what is fashionable and rare right now, not abilities that come easily to amateur collectors, most of whom are better at buying than at selling.

Either way, it's important to know the reason *why* you're collecting and to be honest with yourself about it. Collecting watches may be a good investment or a handy "hedge against inflation," but in order to make this approach work for you, you need to buy the watches that collectors most covet and want (and at the right prices—overpaying eats into your profit), and you need to sell when the time is right. In short, you need exactly the same discipline and knowledge of the marketplace that you'd need in any other area of investment, bearing in mind that, as in most of the art world, the experts are the guys at the auction houses and the galleries who study the prices and values of watches day in, day out, whereas most of the collectors remain amateurs, especially when it comes to estimating the watch market. That is, you are likely to be buying *from* and selling *to* people who know more about the value of the object (and about its potential for rapid sale) than you do—not exactly the ideal situation for an investor.

If I weren't committed to a certain kind of Patek Philippe pocket watch, I think I would set out to learn as much about American watches of the nineteenth century as I could and try to collect items of genuine and distinctive quality—railway watches, for example, with some kind of history. Many of these nineteenth- and early twentieth-century American watches are of unsurpassable quality and were made in every conceivable grade, shape, and style. Or I'd concentrate on a single Swiss maker of quality, perhaps one that isn't already sky-high in prices like Patek—Longines, for example—and try to collect interesting, mint-condition pieces that give some idea of the company's development and innovations over the years—Longines' aviator watches of the 1930s, for example, are unique, and many of their pocket watches are wonderful pieces.

Very thin watches, some of them aptly described as "knife-edged," are a fascinating speciality. They were, in their day, vastly more expensive because of the difficulty of building a very thin movement, particularly if complications are present. Today, many of them are undervalued, even though they represent amazing watchmaking ingenuity and style.

I've seen marvelous collections of antique watchmaking machinery, and lots of it comes up for sale at auctions. Strictly speaking, of course, these machines aren't watches, but they would make a nice accessory or background to a good watch collection.

The choice of what to collect is almost infinite and, of course, deeply personal. The main thing, however, is that the collection, whether large or small, has to give you great pleasure, that there has to be a real satisfaction when you pick up these objects, wind them, wear them, and use them, a sort of inner peace that comes over you when you lay them out in front of you. If they don't do that for you, then why bother, after all?

Before beginning your collection or before deciding what it will include, you should bear in mind the following points:

WOMEN'S WATCHES

You will see a great many women's watches for sale, many from the very greatest manufacturers, but in general, although the fancy women's watches of the 1930s and 1940s are very often extraordinary and ingenious, those of even the most expensive makers such as Patek go for very low prices today. There are several reasons for this, but the most probable explanations are: (1) that mostly men collect watches, and they can't wear a woman's watch; (2) that women's watches far more than men's are pieces of jewelry and therefore subject to the first law of fashion, which is that nobody wants anything that looks out of date or like something their mother used to wear; and (3) that the movements in most of these women's watches are not particularly interesting, except for their small size. For the young women today who prefer to wear a man's sport watch, the gold and diamond-studded dress watches that their mothers or grandmothers wore seem even more dated and out of style. This is a shame, because many women's watches are striking pieces of jewelry, but this trend seems unlikely to change. If you're interested in jewelry per se, a collection of them might be interesting but would probably remain very special and unlikely to appreciate much in value, though you never know.

EARLY ROLEX WATCHES

Early Rolex watches (and by "early" I mean from before the date when they became known most particularly for their underwater ability) are fascinating because the sheer diversity of design and form of the pre-Oyster Rolex watches makes it almost impossible for them not to keep on going up in value, and because no two seem exactly alike and their designs are often astonishingly innovative, it's the kind of collecting that could keep you interested for years. Also, unlike women's fancy watches, you can wear the early Rolex watches, many of which have much more interesting cases and dials (or "faces" as I like to think of them) than any contemporary watch, including those from Rolex.

CARTIER

Think hard about Cartier, which is both a great and a living name in jewelry, with a long tradition behind it. Cartier never made their own movements for watches, but many of the Cartier watches from the 1920s and the 1930s reached a level of design and elegance that remains unequalled; indeed, they seldom look like anybody else's watches. Some of their pocket watches were simply breathtaking in design, and many of their early wristwatches were spectacular, in the full meaning of that word, and are still being copied today by other makers—not least by Cartier itself in its new role as part of an international luxury goods conglomerate. A collection of the many different variations of the famous Cartier "tank watch," for example—the watch that convinced a whole generation of men to give up their pocket watches for the wristwatch—would seem like a wonderful goal, at any rate for a collector with patience and well-lined pockets. Also, books on Cartier abound, full of all the information you need to know and to collect, and *la maison* Cartier is singularly helpful about its history. One thing to note, however, is that the most interesting designs came from Cartier in Paris;

a slight, but significant value attaches to "Cartier, Paris," as opposed to "Cartier, New York," or "Cartier, London."

THINK SWISS

Study the Swiss watchmakers. Plenty of Swiss firms were once famous and widely respected all over the world and are now out of fashion or parts of some larger corporate identity or merely nameplates for watches whose movements are made by others. There was a time, however, when Ulysse Nardin, to take one example, was a name that compared with Patek Philippe or Vacheron & Constantin, and their pre-World War I pocket watches and pre-World War II wristwatches were of the highest quality and often of great elegance of design. The same was true to a greater or lesser degree of such makers as Longines, Audemars Piguet, Girard-Perregaux, Jaeger-LeCoultre, Universal Geneve, Omega, IWC, and numerous others, not to speak of makers of less expensive watches such as Tissot, Zenith, and Movado. Until the temporary collapse of the Swiss watchmaking industry in the face of Japanese competition (as well as the advent of the quartz movement and the flood of cheap digital watches), there were a remarkable number of first-rate Swiss watchmakers, all of them turning out quite distinctive products with their own "look," so much so that a visit to a Swiss watch store in the 1950s and 1960s was a bewildering experience—an *embarras de richesse,* as it were, that made it hard to choose what you wanted. Themes for collecting watches of this period—by manufacturer, by type of watch, by complications—abound, of course, particularly because at that time watches were still being made with relatively old-fashioned faces to satisfy older customers and with much more modern faces to attract the young.

THE *NOUVELLE VAGUE*

A glance at the new designers and manufacturers of watches would be worthwhile as the basis for beginning a collection. F. P. Journe (complicated movements); Daniel Roth (innovative design); Parmigiani (outstanding elegance of design as well as complicated and highly decorated original movements); Alain Silberstein (futuristic design)—all these and many more constitute a new wave of watchmaking, very often pushing beyond the envelope of traditional design to produce objects of great artistic interest and of unique horological innovation. Of course, these watches are not necessarily everybody's cup of tea (though personally I find F. P. Journe's watches interesting and Parmigiani's very handsome indeed), but because they are very special and made mostly in small numbers—indeed, to a degree, many of these watches are pretty much custom-made and already designed with the collector in mind—they are very obviously an attractive possibility for collecting, though not a cheap one. However, it might be more rewarding to pursue them than to be among all those people who bid vast amounts of money for every Patek chronograph wristwatch that comes up for auction. Why be one of the crowd, after all, even if it's a pretty rich crowd?

"DIAMONDS ARE A GIRL'S BEST FRIEND"

Despite Carol Channing and Marilyn Monroe's trademark renditions of this song on stage and screen, it's my general impression that diamonds do not add much to the value or rarity of a watch, certainly when it comes to men's watches. Some of the high-end men's wristwatches with diamond *bâtons* to mark the numbers on the dial are discreetly handsome

The "Bao Dai Rolex," an 18kt gold watch made for the Emperor Bao Dai of Vietnam in 1952, with a special dial with diamond indices.
(Photo courtesy of Phillips, de Pury & Luxembourg)

and look very good with formal wear, but watches swathed in diamonds tend to make the wearer look like a drug dealer and, from a collector's point of view, don't do anything much for the watch. I also strongly suspect that the best quality and grade of diamonds aren't used to decorate watches—Who would notice or care how good they are when used as decoration for a watch?—so they aren't even likely to be worth all that much as stones, either. Better to spend money on classic design, real quality, and mint condition.

PROVENANCE

Whenever a watch's value depends on the identity of its original owner or on the authenticity of some special feature, you need paper—letters, bill of sale, proof that it's genuine. Most of the major makers will provide, on demand (and for a fee), information on when the watch was manufactured and on any special features included when it was made. In the case of watches that were awarded special prizes, such as a high rating at the annual Observatory of Geneva timing contest, the original timekeeping sheets should be available and "part of the package." It should be the seller's job to prove that what you're buying is genuine, not a research job for you to undertake *after* you've bought it.

STRAPS AND BRACELETS

With very rare exceptions, leather straps and metal bracelets add nothing to the value of a wristwatch. Most collectors replace the existing leather strap on a wristwatch with a new one as soon as they've bought it. The important thing to keep in mind, however, is that the little buckle on the strap of wristwatches of high quality ought to be made of the same material as the case of the watch (e.g., made of platinum on a platinum watch) and stamped with the maker's name—in other words, it should be original. Matching, original buckles are hard to find and enormously expensive to replace, so don't suppose that this detail doesn't matter— to collectors, it matters a great deal. Metal bracelets are OK *if* they're original; that is, if the watch originally came from the manufacturer with an integral metal bracelet—of the same metal as the watch case and stamped by the manufacturer. Although less important, if the watch comes with a box or case, it needs to be the *original* one, with the original bill of sale when possible.

Most pocket watches were sold without a chain, but for certain kinds of watches—decorated evening watches, for example—the chain was made to match the watch and should be present, correct (of the same material and pattern of decoration) and marked by the maker.

Pocket watches made before the 1860s, when Breguet and Patek invented the modern winding mechanism of a crown that pulls out to wind, required a key to wind them, and it was usual to carry this key on the watch chain. It should be present. Finding replacement keys is easy enough, but the originals were gold and decorated to match the watch.

In general, the closer a watch is to the state in which it was originally sold—together with all the bits and pieces that accompanied it—the better, but of course the older the watch, the less common this is. Still, originality matters more than anything and is another reason why paperwork, when available, counts.

7

Pitfalls and Forgeries

$\mathcal{W}$ ITH OLDER watches, while there's nothing wrong with their having been restored at some point, some care needs to be taken to define what *restoration* means, and where the limits lie.

A watch with a restored dial or with replacement hands or with a movement that shows signs of careless repair (scratches, distorted slots in the screw heads—known universally throughout the mechanical world as "buggered screw heads"), or with replacement parts that don't have the finish of the original simply isn't as valuable as the same watch in the original condition. In some cases, this kind of thing can be overlooked—a unique and interesting watch that fills an important place in your collection may not be available in a better state, after all—but it should cost less to buy, and eventually it may turn out to be much harder to sell. *Condition always matters.*

It's also worth noting that restoration can go too far. These days it is possible to re-create even quite complex damaged parts and to bring the watch back to "as new" state, but the result may be a watch that is no longer completely original in any real sense; with new interior parts, a restored dial, and new hands, for example, it may *look* good, but it is hardly "original." A skilled appraiser of watches can recognize these signs, as can really knowledgeable collectors, and it's worth learning something about restoration from them if you're going to be serious about collecting.

It is, in fact, possible to ruin a valuable timepiece by *over-restoring* it, first of all because the patina of age and wear has been sacrificed in an attempt to make it look like new and also because in many cases the finish may be better, or at any rate *shinier,* than it was when it left the factory. Watchmakers, however august and distinguished, aim to make a profit on every watch, and they therefore don't waste time polishing to a perfect mirror finish those parts of the watch that you're never going to see or that aren't directly in contact with each other, whereas restorers are apt to polish everything, removing all the tool marks and machining marks left there by the watchmaker. This kind of overkill also results in the blurring of finely engraved numbers or the manufacturer's name on the movement or the case—usually a clear giveaway that somebody has been overzealous with the polishing wheel. Apart from the buggered screw heads and scratches that signify a careless repair job, the blurring of fine engraving is a sure sign that the watch has been extensively restored at some point in its life.

It is sensible to be realistic about old watches. People nearly always took good care of them because they were valuable heirlooms, but, on the other hand, an object that's been in daily use for 100 or 150 years is likely to show a few dents, dings, scratches, and areas of wear, however lovingly it was looked after and serviced. These marks ought to add to the charm, not detract from it. A watch that was made in, say, 1880 *ought* to show a few signs of age, unless it has been sitting untouched and unused in a vault, although there is no reason why it shouldn't keep time as accurately as a brand-new watch (and in many cases, much better). Overpolishing to remove light scratches from daily usage is likely to do more harm than good.

Hairline cracks on the enamel dials of old pocket watches, to take another example, are not at all unusual. The enamel dials are beautiful, far nicer than the more sturdy silver dials that replaced them later in the nineteenth century, and have a lovely translucent quality, like fine china, but they are also comparatively delicate. In most cases, it's possible to live with a few hairline cracks because they're likely to show up only if you look for them with a magnifying loupe. By the same token, the original hands are important to preserve—replacements will almost never have quite the same perfect proportions and delicate lines as the originals and will usually be too bright. Obviously, where something *has* to be replaced because it's broken and can't be repaired, it should be, but where that can be avoided, avoid it. The ceaseless pursuit of perfection leads, with old timepieces, to overrestoration, which can be as damaging as neglect.

Full-scale restoration, of course, is sometimes called for and is sometimes worth it with rare and unusual old watches. Many of the best makers will restore their own old watches—Patek has a whole department that does nothing else—but this is a process that takes a very long time, years sometimes, and is very, very expensive. Also, one problem with these factory restorations is that they often go too far in an attempt to make the watch perfect.

Bear in mind the example of car collecting in the 1980s, when Ferrrari prices were rising at a rapid rate and seemed likely to go on rising forever. Ferrari "California" 250GTs were going for $2 million to $3 million, and GTOs—the greatest Ferrari road car—were going for between $10 million and $12 million. Most of these cars had been crashed at one time or another in races or in ordinary driving, and then restored; new owners had modified and repainted them over the years. One result was that it required real detective work to restore one of these cars to its original color and form—that is, as it left the factory—but a second result was the realization that if you could find a car that had been "totaled" in a crash, all you needed from it was the original brass factory ID plate, usually screwed to the chassis, and you could build a perfectly good and *almost* legitimate replica of a car worth several million dollars. The only thing you needed to do was build a new frame, drop in the right engine (the cars that had been raced had multiple engine changes during their lifetime), add all the chassis bits and pieces, then have somebody hammer out a new aluminum body to duplicate the one that was on the car when it originally left the factory, do a bit of painting and some custom upholstery work—and bingo, you had a "California" for sale in "as new" condition. What gave many of these cars away was that they were *too* perfect—they lacked the rust spots on inner surfaces, the rough, unpolished surfaces on parts that the customer wasn't likely to see, the tool marks and machining marks that the factory workers left on what were, in those days, pretty much handmade cars. Still, the fact was that with a serial number and a brass factory ID plate, any number of people in and around Modena, Italy, where the Ferrari factory is, could turn out a pretty acceptable Ferrari in their backstreet workshops.

By the same token, given an authentic serial number and a bare minimum of useable parts in the movement, a skilled "restorer" can re-create a valuable watch. Given the amount of labor involved, such a recreation would rarely be profitable, but some older watches have been so "restored" that not much remains of the original watch, and a great many contemporary wristwatches can be made far more valuable by relatively limited work. Dials, hands, and bezels are easy enough to replace and can be used to upgrade a watch; the key, therefore, is to know enough to ask the basic questions and to see when something just doesn't *look* right. As always, if it seems too good to be true, then the answer is that it probably *isn't* true.

You should either give an object you are thinking of buying a careful visual examination or, better yet, get an expert to do so for you. For example, the Antiquorum auction house, which specializes in collectible timepieces, classifies each item they sell with a useful series of ratings. A typical rating, this one for a Lange & Söhne "Pour Le Mèrite" tourbillon wristwatch, would be as follows:

☐ **41**

A. Lange & Söhne, Glashütte i. SA., Tourbillon "Pour le Mérite", No. 107/150, Ref. 701.011. Produced in a limited edition of 150 examples in 18K gold in the 1990's, with only 15 produced in 18K pink gold. Sold on March 3, 1999. Production of this reference started in 1994.

Extremely fine and very rare, 18K pink gold gentleman's wristwatch with visible one-minute tourbillon regulator, 36 hours power reserve and an 18K pink gold A. Lange & Söhne buckle. Accompanied by a leather fitted box, certificate and an extra 18K pink gold deployant clasp.

C. three-body, solid, polished and brushed, curved straight lugs, transparent case back with 6 screws to view the movement, sapphire crystals. D. black with applied pink gold indexes, auxiliary sunk guilloché silver dials for the seconds and the up-and-down indication, aperture with polished steel bridge to view the tourbillon. "Alpha" pink gold hands. M. Cal. L 902.0 - No. 432, Glashütte three-quarter plate, nickel-silver, movement decorated and engraved by hand, ""fausses côtes"" decoration, 29 jewels including 5 in screw-mounted gold châtons, tourbillon cage bearing 2 diamond endstones, lateral lever escapement with one-minute tourbillon regulator with polished-steel equidistant three-arm carriage, glucydur balance with screws, adjusted to 5 positions, Nivarox balance-spring with overcoil invented by Prof. Strasser, power equalization with chain and fusée, maintaining power and stepped planetary gearing, shock-absorber, self-compensating Breguet balance-spring.
Dial, case and movement signed.
Diam. 38 mm.

$: 70,000 - 90,000
€ : 65,000 - 83,000

C	2	D	2 - 01	M	2		𝒜

The full explanation of the ratings gives some idea of what is involved in ascertaining the condition of a watch:

GRADING SYSTEM GUIDE

The lots described in this catalogue have been carefully examined and valued by Antiquorum's experts and watchmakers, taking into consideration the aesthetical, historical and technical interest, age and rarity, as well as the technology available at the time of production of each timepiece.

For such judgment to be as objective as possible, it must rest on a number of criteria, particularly with regards to the age of a lot. Indeed, a wristwatch of less than 50 years old cannot be judged with the same criteria as a Renaissance watch. This is the reason for which some of the gradings will only qualify for certain types of watches and will never be used for others.

For example, if, as a general rule, watches can be attributed gradings from 1 to 4 for the case, the dial and the movement, watches of less than 100 years old can be given grading 1 (as new), 3 (in very good condition), or 4 (in good condition). The latter, (grading 4), will be followed by one or more grading numbers to justify why the lot cannot be considered "in very good condition". On the other hand, watches over 100 years old, of similar condition, would indeed be considered as "very good" because of their age and would therefore qualify for grading 3. Needless to say, watches over 100 years old, even in the best state of conservation for their age, are unlikely to ever be considered "as new" and would therefore never be eligible for grading 1; for this reason, we have introduced grading 2 (in perfect condition).

At the end of each lot description, before the estimate, you will find a condition report box, with letters and numbers, divided into 3 sections: these are the grades given to the lot with reference to the condition of its case, its dial and hands, and its movement.

To understand the grades shown in the condition report box, consult the Antiquorum Grading System as follows:

C for the case, followed by one or more numbers = condition of case
D for the dial (& hands), followed by one or more numbers = condition of dial & hands
M for the movement, followed by one or more numbers = condition of movement

Next to this condition report box, is an experts' grading box featuring one letter, from 𝒜 to B, as an overall grade. This overall grade is the opinion of Antiquorum's experts, as a global appreciation of the lot, based on its general condition, quality, technical and historical interest, age and rarity. On this basis, it must be understood that a very early timepiece, a prototype or a watch featuring a rare escapement, although it may be in a mediocre state of conservation, enven re-cased or lacking its dial, can qualify for gradings AAA or even 𝒜 .

To understand the grade shown in the experts' grading box, consult the Experts' Overall Opinion.

See example below:

C	1	D	1 - 01	M	1		𝒜

Experts' overall opinion: Exceptional
Movement: as new
Dial: as new - original hands
Case: as new

Antiquorum's Grading System for Timepieces, 2003

CASE (C)

GENERAL REMARKS

1 as new
2 in perfect condition
3 very good
4 good

DETAILS

5 slightly oxydized
6 slightly scratched
7 oxydized
8 scratched
9 deeply scratched
10 a dent
11 dents
12 replacements
13 lacking elements
14 slightly worn
15 worn
16 very worn
17 transformations
18 alterations
19 damaged
20 very damaged
21 slightly restored
22 restorations
23 repolished edges
    preserved
24 repolished edges
    altered
25 back threading
    damaged
26 period original
27 later original
28 period
29 later
30 custom made
31 worn push-piece
32 worn push-pieces
33 replaced push-pieces
34 original crown
35 later original crown
36 period crown
37 to be restored
38 partially re-gilt
39 re-gilt

ENAMEL AND VARIOUS TYPES OF DECORATION

40 slightly scratched
41 scratched
42 hairline
43 hairlines
44 slightly worn
45 worn
46 very worn
47 very slightly chipped
48 chipped
49 damaged
50 very damaged
51 slightly restored
52 restorations
53 period original
54 later original
55 period
56 later
57 custom made
58 to be restored
59 pearl missing
60 pearls missing
61 paste stone missing
62 paste stones missing
63 precious stone missing
64 precious stones missing

DIAL (D)

GENERAL REMARKS

1 as new
2 in perfect condition
3 very good
4 good

ENAMEL AND METAL

5 slightly oxydized
6 slightly scratched
7 oxydized
8 scratched
9 deeply scratched
10 a dent
11 dents
12 hairline
13 two hairlines
14 more than two hairlines
15 chip(s) or hairline(s) under bezel, not visible when closed
16 slightly worn
17 worn
18 very worn
19 very slightly chipped
20 chipped
21 damaged
22 very damaged
23 slightly restored
24 restorations
25 soft overglazed
26 partly rubbed
27 spotted
28 reprinted
29 period, original
30 later original
31 period
32 later
33 custom made
34 to be restored

HANDS

01 original
02 later original
03 partially replaced
04 period
05 later

MOVEMENT (M)

GENERAL REMARKS

1 as new
2 in perfect condition
3 very good
4 good

DETAILS

5 slightly oxydized
6 slightly scratched
7 oxydized
8 scratched
9 rusted
10 a dent
11 dents
12 replacements
13 lacking elements
14 later escapement
15 upgraded
16 later balance
17 transformations
18 alterations
19 damaged
20 very damaged
21 slightly restored
22 restorations
23 inscription rubbed
24 to be overhauled
25 re-gilt
26 period, original
27 later original
28 period
29 later
30 custom made
31 to be restored
    a. cleaned
    b. minor
    c. major
    d. broken staff

* overhaul recommended
   (at buyer's expense)

** overhaul required
   (at buyer's expense)

Experts' Overall Opinion

(GENERAL CONDITION; QUALITY; TECHNICAL AND HISTORICAL INTEREST; AGE; RARITY)

ANTIQUE, VINTAGE AND MODERN TIMEPIECES

ᴧ : Exceptional
AAA: Excellent
AA: Very Good
A: Good
B: Fair

MILITARY WATCHES

AAA: Very rare
AA: Rare
A: Classic

As you can see, from the above, a watch can fall short of the ideal in many ways, some of them difficult for the average amateur collector to pick up on, but all of them meaningful in determining the value of the watch.

There isn't much outright fraud in the watch business, largely because creating a totally fraudulent object that would pass muster as a product of a famous watchmaker—say, Vacheron & Constantin or Audemars Piguet—would be so costly a task that there wouldn't be any real margin for profit, but that doesn't mean that there aren't some doubtful objects floating around the marketplace that have been altered or spruced up or "restored" to increase their value. Hence, the importance of back up. The fact that a watch is inscribed by or to or from a famous person is nice, for example, but there should be some paperwork to support the genuineness of the inscription, in the form of letters, a bill of sale, and so on. An unusual dial or combination of dial and hands may be interesting, but it would be nice to have proof that the watch emerged that way from the factory.

With older pocket watches, there is often some confusion over the case, as opposed to the movement. Here, it is important to understand that U.S. customs duties on completed watches imported from Europe were high enough in the mid-nineteenth century that many jewelers preferred to import watch movements from Switzerland at a far lower duty, then place them in American-made cases. Then, too, many Swiss manufacturers were happy enough to enter the American market by selling their watches under an American jeweler's name—Patek Philippe, for example, had an agreement with Tiffany for many years to sell their watches in America, with the Tiffany name on the dial and the case, although the movement in such watches is sometimes (but by no means always) engraved with Patek Philippe's name, the "Made in Geneva" mark, and the appropriate Patek Philippe serial number. The case, however, would usually bear Tiffany's name and serial number, and the U.S. mark for 18-karat gold—that is, "18KT" as opposed to ".750." At that time, Tiffany was a far more famous name on this side of the Atlantic than Patek Philippe, so the arrangement made sense for both parties.

Here, we again find ourselves in the realm of personal taste. Most collectors prefer that a high-quality watch be "triple signed,"—that is, signed by the manufacturer on the movement, the case, and the dial—and conventional wisdom holds that a watch that *isn't* triple signed is significantly less valuable. However, if you take the example of Patek and Tiffany, the watch cases made by Tiffany are often more solid, better made, more elaborate, and more beautifully decorated than those made in Switzerland, so the so-called Tiffany Pateks, in fact, in the present-day market, may represent something of a bargain for the collector. Certainly the minute-repeater split-second chronograph pocket watch presented to Cornelius Vanderbilt Jr. by his father on his twenty-first birthday that is in my collection would have been way out of my league if it had been triple signed, instead of having the Tiffany name on the dial and case. Besides, it's a piece of U.S. history—U.S. *family* history, anyway—bought for Cornelius Vanderbilt Jr. in the days when Tiffany's name and reputation meant more in America than that of any Swiss watch manufacturer; it was, in fact, a guarantee of quality.

To some extent, this custom lives on. Tiffany & Co. still sells "house brand" watches with the Tiffany name on the dial—although the watches are made in Switzerland for Tiffany—as do other major jewelers, including, but by no means limited to, Cartier, Bvlgari, and Van Cleef & Arpels. In addition, the great jewelers usually place their own name discreetly on the dial of the other watches they sell, so a Rolex bought at the Tiffany watch counter will often have Tiffany's name in tiny letters on the dial somewhere, below (and smaller than) Rolex's own. Jewelers such as Tiffany & Co., Cartier (during the days when they also sold other people's watches, not just their own), Gübelin in Lucerne, Shreve & Co. in San Francisco, Bailey Banks & Biddle Co. in Philadelphia, and others almost always had their own name in tiny letters placed on the dial of every watch they sold, and customers seemed to like the practice, because it added another layer of prestige to an already prestigious purchase or gift. Collectors are harder to please, however, and most of them seem to prefer watches that *don't* have the retailer's name on the dial, though why this should be so beats me.

Expensive Swiss pocket watches of the nineteenth and early twentieth centuries nearly always have the retailer's name and city elaborately engraved on the inside cover (or *cuvette*), together with the serial number. This engraving was usually done at the factory. In some cases, watchmakers went further to please major retailers or important individual clients of the house. For example, I own a hunter-cased Patek minute repeater, manufactured in 1883 and sold in August 1884 to George H. Ford, a respected and very successful jeweler and leading citizen in New Haven, Connecticut, who made a yearly buying trip to Europe; in the course of one trip, he apparently ordered a Patek watch while visiting their show room in Geneva. Because he was one of Patek's major retailers in New England, the watch was given lavish special attention, including an "Extra" movement, and his name was painted on the dial instead of Patek's, no doubt as a compliment to him. It was also engraved on the *cuvette* and even, far more rare, on the *movement* of the watch, in addition to which his initials were elaborately floral engraved on the cover. In short, Patek pulled out all the stops when it came to George H. Ford's personal watch. There is hardly any watch short of a royal one that carries its owner's name in more places or more prominently placed, and it is easy to imagine the pride with which "General" Ford (like most well-to do and influential Americans of the post-Civil War period, he acquired and used a military title, in his case as commissary-general of the state of Connecticut, an honorary gubernatorial appointment) gazed at his watch. He appears to have been a bulky man, with a walrus moustache ending in long, waxed, upturned points like the kaiser's, heavy jowls, and small, piercing eyes. Photographs of him invariably show him as a formidable figure, dressed in a formal frock coat with a rose pinned to one of the satin lapels, a tight and high starched collar, an elegantly tied silk cravat, and of course a waistcoat with a thick gold watch chain stretched over a substantial stomach, the end of it no doubt fastened to the famous Patek Philippe watch. The sight of him drawing it out of his waistcoat pocket and flipping the lid open to stare at it and make sure of the time must have been chilling indeed to those of his employees who were a few seconds late.

Patek did the same for another major retailer, Henry J. Howe, of Syracuse, New York, whose elaborate Victorian Gothic H. J. Howe Building was for many decades a Syracuse landmark. Back in the days when local jewelers were big and prosperous establishments, rivaling Tiffany in New York, Howe sold silverware, wedding gifts, trophies, watches, clocks, objets d'art, and much else besides. The five-story Howe Building with its carved gargoyles, turrets, and stained-glass cathedral windows has gone now, along with much of downtown Syracuse, and of course so has Howe, who served in the Civil War under General McClennan and lived on to 1916. His Patek split-second chronograph with a minute repeater and a thirty-minute counter (pretty much the top of the line), which I now own, was, like that of his fellow jeweler George Ford of New Haven, elaborately marked with Howe's name in every conceivable place and clearly given special attention by the manufacturer.

Others besides major Patek retailers got special treatment, of course. It is important to understand that the watch business, at its higher levels, was and remains a *custom* business— the customer can have whatever he wants (and can pay for). I own a typical example, a pink gold Patek minute-repeater split-second chronograph with a thirty-minute counter, ordered by George M. Jewett, a wealthy Texan, in the late nineteenth century and delivered with the Jewett family crest enameled on the back by the maker, with Jewett's name engraved on the case and the movement, and with a pink gold chain designed to match the watch. The watch was placed in a fitted box of polished rare wood, inlaid with ivory and lined in silk. It must have represented a very substantial investment indeed.

Major clients such as Henry Graves or Warren Packard, founder of the famous motor car company and almost as much of a fanatic about time and collecting watches as his rival Graves, got everything they asked for, including a special serial number, their name engraved on the movement, their coat of arms engraved wherever they liked, and numerous special features, or even one-of-a-kind watches made just for them.

Even in today's much more highly mechanized world, the customer who wants something special and is prepared to wait for it will receive special attention in a quiet, discreet way. Rolex, though it basically mass-produces watches, will make special dials to the customer's request and much else besides—it's only a matter of time and money.

One of the lovelier Rolex special dials, sometimes seen on early models of their waterproof calendar watch with moon phases, has tiny raised stars instead of the conventional numbers and bars, in yellow gold or white gold, depending on the color of the case; these stars, which could be ordered specially, transform an already handsome watch into an exquisite one and raise the value of the watch considerably. In short, even when everybody swears that a certain manufacturer would never have produced a watch with this or that special feature, the fact remains that they may perfectly well have done so for a good customer or for one who was prepared to pay for something different.

A comparison might be to Porsche A. G., which makes expensive sports cars with a wide list of options but maintains a special customer services department for "old clients" of the company who have bought many Porsches or those who are simply very rich, and want something unique and special that *can't* be found on the options sheet—hand-sewn kangaroo leather upholstery, perhaps, or rosewood veneer interior trim or dials with Arabic numerals or a built-in refrigerator, not to speak of colors and engine modifications that aren't available to the normal buyer. Watchmakers, too, like to keep in place a few custom craftsmen who can meet any requirement from a customer, however expensive, bizarre, or unique.

Historically, the major Swiss manufacturers were also in no hurry to sell their wares, in particular the movements with *grandes complications,* which were expensive and time-consuming to produce, often lacked customers who could afford to buy them, or had been made on special order for somebody who died before they could be completed. These movements therefore sat on the shelf until the right customer came along—the most respected watch manufacturers could afford to be patient, after all. Thus, it is not by any means uncommon to find perpetual calendar watches with movements that were begun in the nineteenth century but were not cased and sold until well into the twentieth century, with the result that many of the most modern-looking cases in fact contain movements made twenty, thirty, or more years earlier.

In addition, during the period of transition between the pocket watch and the wristwatch some of the smaller movements made for pocket watches were kept for long periods of time, then ingeniously inserted into wristwatch cases to meet the new demand. Watch manufacturers are in the luxury trade, of course, but most of them are also Swiss, which is to say thrifty and cautious, and seldom discard anything they have made, however long ago.

Another reason for this kind of disparity in the age of watch parts lies in the fact that the technology of traditional watches hasn't made any sort of quantum leap in the past hundred years or more. Computerization, standardization of parts, and sophisticated miniature machine tools have made it easier (and less expensive) to produce finer watch movements than those that were hand assembled of hand-finished parts before World War II, and, of course, to produce watches more quickly and in larger quantity than ever before. Still, very few watches made today, if any, exceed in complexity, finish, or accuracy those made by Breguet in the late eighteenth century with hand tools, and most of the *grandes complications* on which watch manufacturers still pride themselves were available to well-heeled customers more than a century ago—the split-second chronograph with registers, the minute repeater, the perpetual calendar with moon phases—none of these things is *new*.

This being the case, it is hardly surprising that movements made a generation or two earlier can be placed in an up-to-date case and perform faultlessly. This disparity between the manufacturing date of the movement and that of the case, however, emphasizes the need to look into the history of the watch and to have as much supporting evidence as you can assemble that it is what it appears to be.

Most of the older watch manufacturers keep some kind of an archive or historical service, though not all of them are very responsive to queries from watch collectors. On the other hand, the example of Patek—which not only has its own museum, but issues, on request and for a modest fee, "Extracts from Archives," giving all the details of any watch they have manufactured—has led to a change in attitude on the subject of collecting. Until a few years ago, most of the manufacturers were more interested in selling you a new watch than in answering enquiries about old ones, but it soon dawned on most of them that their past is, to some degree, their present and future, that the desirability of the contemporary product is in part triggered by the reputation for quality and elegance of the products of the past. Thus, though the current Breguet company and their products have hardly more than a tenuous connection to Breguet of the eighteenth century, they have cleverly managed to link the two in the buyer's mind, in part by borrowing from Abraham-Louis Breguet's instantly recognizable style of design and adapting it to wristwatches, and in part by using their past to promote their present product line. Patek has been doing the same for years with great success, and Vacheron & Constantin is not far behind. One result is to make collecting the vintage watches of a given manufacturer a topic toward which the company is more or less obliged to behave respectfully; another is that most major manufacturers have followed Patek's lead and created their own museum. This is, to put it bluntly, good for collectors. Admittedly, it means that in many cases the highest bidder at auctions may turn out to be the manufacturer of the watch, acquiring the piece for its museum, but it also means that in the case of interesting or important pieces, the manufacturer is setting a "floor" price on the grounds that if their old (that is, vintage) watches go for good prices, people will be that much more likely to buy their contemporary watches in the stores.

Your three best resources in collecting are (1) the historian or the person in charge of the archives at the company that made the watch, (2) the record of auction sales of similar or identical watches, and (3) the sales brochures of the company that made the watch. The last, by the way, is a major subject in itself, because people collect these brochures, too, but when they can be found, they are of enormous help, particularly with companies that sold an almost infinite variety of styles. Generally speaking, this held true for most watch companies from World War I to World War II, when even smaller manufacturers went in for dozens of different case shapes, lug styles, and dials. American watch companies such as Gruen, Bulova, and Hamilton carried this diversity to extraordinary degrees, once the wristwatch became accepted wear for men, because they could use what was basically a single, relatively inexpensive movement to produce a bewildering variety of styles, in every kind of material and at every price range, from stainless steel to gold plate and even gold. What's more, like American automobile manufacturers of the period, they changed styles constantly, promoting their watches as fashion items rather than as potential heirlooms, so their product line always looked new and up to date in jewelers' display counters (and so that the one you were wearing, of course, looked "old-fashioned"). It's hard to imagine how even their own sales forces could keep track of all the different models and styles they made. This approach, however, helps to explain why hardly any two popularly priced American watches made in the years between the wars look alike.

And that's just *men's* watches, of course—women's watches were even more fashion-driven. The sales brochures can help you pinpoint when the watch was made, if it is genuine or not, and what the model number was, so if you're thinking of starting a collection of wristwatches built around a single company, whether Swiss or American, it would be a good idea to begin by building up a collection of the company's sales brochures over the years, plus all the books you can find that have been written about the company in question. There is hardly any Swiss, American, or German watch company to which someone has not at some time devoted a long and detailed book, full of exactly the kind of information you're going to need. I have before me, as I write, an enormous book on Cartier watches, another on Breguets (historic and modern), four on Rolexes, and six on Patek Philippes. Each is big-format, heavily illustrated, and weighs a ton. On the other hand, if you've got a watch in your hand (or on your mind as an acquisition) and want to know whether it was originally manufactured with a metal bracelet instead of a strap as an option or whether the dial was peculiar to this model or what year it was manufactured, the information is more than likely going to be in these books.

In some cases, as with early Rolex watches, even tiny differences can mean the difference between a valuable collector's item and a nice but ordinary watch—the Paul Newman Daytona chronographs are only one example of many, and studying the brochures is the best way to identify a watch for sure.

Thus, building up your personal library on the watch of your choice is an essential first step to collecting and the best way to assure yourself that what you're buying was, in fact, available from the factory just as it is and that you're not looking at a watch that has been significantly altered to make it more interesting to the collector.

Better to read about the watch before buying than to read about it after you've bought it and discover that what you've got isn't exactly what you thought it was!

8

From the Sublime to the Ridiculous

NE OF the liberating things about collecting is that somebody out there is collecting more improbable objects than you are (and spending more money on them). Almost everybody who collects—who collects *anything*—believes at heart that he or she is acting sensibly and prudently, making a wise investment in objects that can only go up in value because of their rarity and beauty, even if they *do* happen to consist of the heads of the major twentieth-century world figures hand carved on walnut shells. I have rarely, if ever, met a collector who didn't feel that his or her collection made sense, financially and aesthetically, whether it consists of Elvis Presley coffee mugs or impressionist paintings.

The late Malcolm Forbes, a friend of mine—I edited and published many of his books—was an omnivorous collector, possibly the most omnivorous I have ever met. Old-fashioned windup toys (among thousands of toys, he had a whole fleet of windup battleships from his own childhood, some of them big enough to fill half the bath tub, which just goes to reinforce my belief that the collecting spirit begins early in life and that no real collector ever throws anything away), Fabergé eggs (his collection was second only to that of Queen Elizabeth II), cars (both vintage and modern), motorcycles, the gowns and caps of all his honorary degrees (which filled a whole wall-size display case), wine, the letters and signatures of famous people through the ages, jewelry, hot-air balloons, Scottish paraphernalia, there was simply no end to the amount or range of Malcolm's collecting. It was as if he could never be content with *one* of anything.

Of course, Malcolm spent a fortune collecting, but I learned a lot about collecting from him, despite the significant difference in the amount of money we could spend to indulge our collecting appetites. The most important thing was that Malcolm had a great time collecting—collecting gave him real pleasure, whether he was bidding successfully for bottles of Thomas Jefferson's Madeira wine (and later, serving it to his friends) or finding a windup toy he didn't have. Collecting things should be a *pleasure*—it should be *fun*—an activity you enjoy, and the things you collect should give you a deep, personal sense of satisfaction. Malcolm also *learned* by collecting. Whether it was about motorcycles or art, he soaked up information, sought out experts, and read every book on the subject—he became, in short, an expert himself (without, let it be said, ever becoming a bore). And he didn't hoard or hide his collections; he wanted them to give pleasure to other people as well—he wanted people to *share* his pleasure and to get as much enjoyment out of his collections as he did. He was emphatically not a "Don't touch it!" kind of collector. If you admired one of his toys, he unlocked the display case and wound it up for you, then got down on his hands and knees with you to show you how it worked. If you admired one of his Fabergé eggs, he took it out from its case so you could fondle it. If you liked one of his cars, he had it taken out and drove you in it or even let you drive it.

I have often thought of him when I see people collecting watches, locking them away in vaults, never wearing them, never giving other people a chance to admire them, buying them solely as an investment, without developing or communicating any passion for the art and science of time measurement or educating themselves about what they own.

Of course, watches are valuable objects, and it makes sense to secure them, but at the same time, however valuable they may be, they are meant to be used, worn, displayed. As Zero Mostel shouts in Mel Brooks's *The Producers,* "That's it, baby, if you've got it, *flaunt* it!"

People are always surprised that I use and wear my pocket watches, but their surprise surprises me. What else would I do with them? How much pleasure would they give me shut up in a locked drawer at home? I like the thought that a part of my collection is in my waistcoat pocket, that it's ticking away reliably, and that I can, when I choose, pull it out of my pocket to see what the time is and show it off to people. Even people who *aren't* interested in watches are usually fascinated by the chiming of a minute repeater and enjoy hearing something of the watch's history, who owned it, and why it was special to them.

When I'm home, I always keep a few on my desk, enjoying the sight of them, and measuring their accuracy by my very modern Patek Philippe Naviquartz ship's chronometer in its polished, glass-topped wooden box. If I'm bored or restless or tired, I pick one up, admire it, remind myself how old it is, how many people it has belonged to, and on how many other desks and bedside tables it was no doubt placed with due care in the past 120 years or so since it was manufactured. Our Victorian and Edwardian ancestors (those who could afford a good watch) usually had a small watch stand about six inches high on the table by their bed so that the last thing they did at night before turning out the light was to wind up their watch—ever so gently and precisely—then hang it by its bow from a hook on the stand. That way, they could turn on the light and see what time it was if they woke up during the night; they could also make sure that they weren't leaving the watch in the clutter of other, less valuable objects, with the risk that they might knock it off the table to the floor. (One advantage to minute-repeater watches was that you didn't need to light a candle to know what time it was—you just reached out and pushed the button to sound the chimes.) I have one watch stand in the shape of a bronze eagle, wings outstretched, with a hook in its beak from which a watch can be suspended, and another in polished wood and gilded brass, given to me by my dear friends Avi and Sidney Offit, with a handy little cup carved in the wooden base, in which you can place your cuff links, studs, and tie pin overnight. Very handy.

The idea of keeping a pocket watch suspended in the vertical position is, in any case, an old, established one. You can see the dial that way, whereas if it's lying flat and you're in bed, you can't. In addition there is an old wive's tale that watches generally keep time more accurately if they're in the vertical position, because the very small amount of lubricating oil in the watch tends to drip downward through the works of the watch, then is carried back up again through the works as the gears rotate. This is doubtful—marine chronometers were always kept flat in the horizontal position—but there are even true believers (as a former Swiss schoolboy, I know that Switzerland is full of them) who make sure that their *wristwatch* is in the upright position at night—you can do that by manipulating the watch band or bracelet to act rather like a small easel to support the case. I will confess here and now that I wear my one and only wristwatch, an indestructible Rolex (which has been with me through the Royal Air Force and the 1956 Hungarian Revolution, and much else), on my wrist at night because Rolex and Omega are the only top of the line manufacturers, in my experience, who make luminous dials that are virtually bright enough to read by, so I just have to glance at it in the dark to know what time it is—and despite this it always keeps perfect time.

Sometimes it seems to me that large numbers of people—judging by eBay, about half the population of the United States—are desperately in search of something to collect and willing to make a collection out of pretty much anything. Collecting fountain pens, for example, went from being esoteric to upscale and widespread in less than a decade. Only a few years ago, old fountain pens were essentially worthless junk; then as people looked around for an accessory that they could use in everyday business and personal life and that could also draw attention to their taste, their enjoyment of the finer things of life, and their willingness to write long-hand in real ink instead of on a word processor or with a throwaway felt tip or ballpoint pen, old fountain pens sky-rocketed in value. Pen manufacturers turned to making collectible fountain pens, elaborately decorated and packaged, that sold for thousands of dollars in the fancier stationery shops, though the real connoisseurs preferred the old Parkers and Watermans from the 1920s or 1930s. The thing about collecting fountain pens (apart from the fact that it tends to lead to an improvement in your handwriting) is that if you have to carry *some* kind of pen, you may as well at least have an interesting and unique one, and once you give in to the collector's instinct, you can carry a different one every day. Pen collectors go in for quantity in a big way, to judge by the elaborate wooden display cases with lined drawers that take a dozen pens each, and I know several people who have dozens of pens. I myself, sitting at my desk, can count nine fountain pens within sight, and I don't even consider myself a pen collector.

Reading a magazine such as *Robb's Report* (which you can pick up for free on the Boston or Washington shuttles) has a certain dizzying effect on me. Here are people collecting juke boxes, Western boots, model airplanes, antique telephones, beer mugs, cattle brands, swords, ship models—you name it. I have a friend who collects only items retrieved from sunken ships—china, glassware, silverware, ashtrays; if it hasn't been brought up from some liner that's been on the ocean bottom for fifty years or so, he isn't interested. Compared to much of this collecting, watch collecting seems sensible and, if done with some judgment and taste, a sensible investment as well; watches are interesting objects, too—

complex, full of tricky and even astonishing inventions, perhaps the most familiar and everyday proof of human ingenuity and our capacity for mechanical genius.

When you look at the inner workings of a watch, you cannot help but be amazed. Who first invented and made these tiny, coiled springs, thinner than the thinnest airmail paper, but durable enough to last for one or two centuries of use? Who managed, before the age of precision machine tools, to make these tiny, polished screws, each one perfect, half a dozen of them no bigger than a grain of rice? Who first imagined the tiny concentric circles, operating within the crowded case of a watch, that bring the date, the day of the week, and the month clicking into view on the dial in their little rectangular openings, or the complex mechanism that on some watches makes the seconds hand click every second rather than going around in continuous sweep—a "jumping" or "dead" second hand, as it is called? We humans are never more God-like than in the machines we invent, and in the watch, we have created as close as we will ever come to our own tiny version of the Cosmos. Even the cheapest of mechanical watches is an amazing mechanism—doubly amazing, perhaps, because it can be mass-produced and sold for such a low price.

It's for this reason that collecting watches need not necessarily cost a fortune—a good many of the cheaper ones are, in their own way, just as interesting and collectible as the multimillion dollar ones. If you look back at the catalogs of many of the lower-priced watch companies over the years, you'll be amazed at how diverse and varied their production has been (not to speak of indestructible—I gave my stepfather John Astarita a Tissot watch way back in the late 1940s; it wasn't new then or expensive, but it is still keeping perfect time on his wrist today). Masses of watches made by Swiss and American watch firms between the wars are still out there, many with dials and cases that seem striking and innovative even now. A collection of stainless steel sports watches would have a lot of potential, I think, many of them having been made in the days when stainless steel was still considered an exotic material. Even today, stainless steel has its own special charm for collectors. Patek wristwatches in stainless steel very often sell for more than the same model would in gold or platinum, because Patek so rarely used stainless steel for their best watches, and Rolex chronographs in stainless steel very often sell for more at auction than the same watch in 18-karat gold. What's more, women have come to prefer stainless steel men's watches, with stainless steel bracelets, to more expensive gold watches on the grounds that they look "sportier" and more casual, less like jewelry.

The Soviet watch industry, in its day, turned out untold millions of watches, most of them inexpensive. They show up often at watch shows and even at auctions these days, and are being vigorously collected. Many of them commemorate Soviet space achievements or astronauts, and others have purported Soviet military markings and decorations. Most of the latter are almost certainly spurious, manufactured after the dissolution of the USSR with Western collectors in mind, but occasionally a genuine military timepiece comes up for sale, including some interesting naval chronographs, deck watches, and what appears to be the Soviet Air Force's entire supply of aircraft clocks. Some of the military equipment demonstrates the degree to which the Soviet Union could manufacture objects of quality and durability when they had a mind to—mostly in the technical and military sphere, as opposed to the consumer one.

Anything out of the ordinary like this may provide the basis for an interesting specialized collection at a comparatively low cost—as well as providing any number of interesting puzzles to be solved in identifying who manufactured what and for what purpose. Even the collecting of something as specialized as American military pocket watches of World War II would provide enough order numbers, serial numbers, unit and service ID numbers, and so on to keep you busy for years. When was the item ordered, by whom, in what quantity, and for which service and to which units or vessels was it supplied? These are among the questions which are raised by these very handsome pocket watches, most of them in stainless steel, for the use of the artillery and the air force, and researching the answers would give a great additional interest to the collection.

All sorts of timepieces are out there in great quantity. Many aren't all that expensive, but have all the attributes that make for a fine collection. As in most collecting, part of the challenge is pursuing the exact history and identity of a piece and identifying what that makes it unusual or special. There is, in effect, a *learning process* to watch collecting, at whatever level, and the learning process is part of the fun, part of the reason for collecting in the first place. It may not take all that much knowledge to buy the big items for six or seven figures at the major auctions—in the first place, for watches of this caliber, the research has already been done, and, in the second place, they wouldn't be selling for this kind of money if they weren't the real thing—but at lower levels of value it is your knowledge that will give you an edge and tell you which items to buy and which to reject.

Whether the object is sublime or ridiculous, you have to become your own expert, and be able to recognize what makes a watch something out of the ordinary that belongs in your collection, even if what you're collecting is Mickey Mouse watches (actually quite a lively field). Collecting isn't about money, or it shouldn't be—it's about *knowledge,* and what matters is having a collection of objects that are special, interesting, in some way unique, that you know more about than most people do, and that give you, for whatever reason, a certain pleasure to own. What the objects cost you or what they could some day be sold for ought not to be the question, nor should you ever think that because somebody else's collection is larger or more expensive, it must therefore be better or more significant.

A collection might be made (at no great expense) of watches as jewelry, for example. By the turn of the previous century, when watch movements were successfully "miniaturized" (a word that did not yet exist), tiny watches became incorporated into money clips, cigar cutters, cuff links, cigarette lighters, tie clips, fountain pens, and almost anything else that a man might carry, thus freeing the gentleman of fashion from wearing a watch on his wrist or from carrying one in his waistcoat pocket (at just the moment when men were starting, in any case, to give up the waistcoat). For the ladies, tiny watches were built into cigarette cases, the clips of handbags, brooches, and even lorgnettes and the handles of fans (thus permitting women to look at the time while watching an opera or a ballet and gauge how far distant dinner or an entr'acte might be). Much of this miniaturization had been done earlier, in the eighteenth and nineteenth centuries, at least so far as ladies' fans and lorgnettes were concerned, but the new, mass-produced movements were no longer expensive horological triumphs. These tiny watches, many of them made by the European Watch Company for Cartier, now sell for virtually nothing—they have been reduced to curiosities—but a collection of them would be fascinating, and many of them were installed in *objets de luxe* by the great jewelry houses.

My mother owns a Cartier (Paris) woman's wristwatch from the mid-1930s, a gift from my father, who despite never wearing a watch himself had an excellent eye for this kind of thing, consisting of a slim, articulated bracelet—like a snake it bends in all directions, each link a tiny, paper-thin, polished half circle of gold—and a watch so small that you have to look hard to see that it's there and harder still, alas, to read the time. It's a work of stunning originality and beauty, one of a kind (I've certainly never seen another one like it), but probably these days not worth nearly as much as it cost. The fashion for this kind of "dress" watch died out in the 1950s, but my guess is that a collection of similar pieces from the great jewelers of the period would almost certainly come back into fashion at some point and in the meantime would give the owner a great deal of pleasure as well as an interesting amount of research to do—Who designed the piece, who ordered it for whom? In many cases, Cartier and other jewelers made decorative watches as one-of-a-kind objects, either on spec, confident that somebody would buy it, or on special order from a customer who was looking for something unique and original. After some discussion, Cartier would present the customer with sketches from their design department, and once the customer made a final selection and paid a deposit, they then manufactured the piece in their own workshops. Some of these sketches, many of which appear in the various books on Cartier, are as interesting as the final product itself, small works of art that portray brilliant design, faultless engineering (Cartier's hinges alone are tiny masterpieces), and an enormously imaginative use of precious metals, semiprecious materials, and precious stones. Those who follow auctions will know that these hybrids—jewelry and timepiece combined—now go for less than they are worth, so even if you can't wear them, they may still be worth acquiring as the basis for an unusual collection. It would be particularly interesting to get a copy of the bill of sale and of the original design department's sketches for a decorative piece, neither of which is impossibly difficult to do with those major jewelers who are still in business (and most are).

In a recent auction catalog, two pieces caught my eye, neither of them particularly expensive, both certainly collectible. One was a Movado Ermerto purse watch, which was a popular item among men and women when I was at school. It's a little, rectangular clock/watch, leather covered, with smooth edges and ends, so it can easily be carried in the pocket. It opens up to reveal a handsome little triple-date calendar watch with phases of the moon and winds itself every time you open and close it. These watches were made in every imaginable sort of finish, from lacquer to leather to textured gold, and with many different kinds of movement, including one with an alarm clock. Though unique and handsome, they go for relatively low prices. They all have a clever little easel that springs up at the touch of a fingernail so you can use one as a bedside clock at night. Most of them show a good deal of wear on the outside, because they tended to get carried in the pocket or purse with change or keys, but that somehow makes them even more interesting.

The other piece was a stainless steel Cartier wristwatch with the *reversible basculante,* Cartier's answer to Jaeger-LeCoultre's Reverso watch, except that the watch can be swiveled upright, so it can either be worn on the wrist conventionally or propped up vertically on the night table as a clock. Again, not a very expensive piece, but it might be fun to collect all the different wristwatches in which the watch itself swivels or can be positioned in several ways. Hamilton Watch Co. in the United States made one that is as nice as anything from Cartier or Jaeger-LeCoultre, and plenty of others approached the idea with various patented solutions of their own. A nice field for collecting, I would say—maybe not for me, but for you?

9
Ownership

*T*HE MOST important thing to remember about collecting is that we don't ever truly "own" a collection—we merely take care of it during the time it's in our hands, then pass it on. Few collections of *anything*, however valuable, escape the changes of ownership, the outright destruction, or the dispersement that time brings about. Works of art in the collections of popes, kings, and princes were lost, refound, sold, dispersed, and eventually made their way across the Atlantic to a continent that was still unknown when they were executed, to enter the collections of men such as J. P. Morgan, and, from him, eventually into the Metropolitan Museum of Art.

No matter how carefully you try to protect a collection, you can't plan for or legislate the future. When collectors die, their widows or children will more than likely sell off the collection; high estate taxes, war, revolution, occupation, or holocaust will have had the same effect, whisking valuables out of the hands of those who own them and sending them on an unpredictable path into the hands of strangers. Most older valuable watches, with rare exceptions, have been through many, many hands since they were first bought, and before they reach yours. Lost, stolen, recovered, sold, and sold again, hardly any watch more than one hundred years old does not have a story behind it.

With that simple truth in mind, it becomes obvious that however strong our pride of possession may be, we don't own anything worth collecting, but merely hold it in trust, as it were, restoring, classifying, and safeguarding it for the next generation. Because so many watches were cased in gold, they have always been recognized as valuable, and because they serve an obviously and universally recognized useful purpose—keeping time—they are seldom broken up and melted down just for their gold. The watch is generally more valuable as an object than the gold it contains, unlike wedding rings, much jewelry, gold plate, and gold dental fillings.

Even during the most intense period of the Holocaust, victims' watches were carefully registered, appraised, and inspected by teams of Jewish watchmaker-prisoners, then "redistributed" within Germany by the SS, as opposed to being melted down for their gold. Hardly any object is more likely to survive in extreme conditions of social and political stress than a good watch, though it is, of course, very likely to change hands as the winners take it from the losers.

For years (before I decided to limit myself to Patek Philippe pocket watches), I owned a very nice gold hunter by Jules Jurgensen, in beautiful condition, with the name of a well-known and elegant Warsaw jeweler engraved on the *cuvette*. One of the things that made it special for me—nobody else seemed to have noticed—was that on the inside of the cover, along with the case serial number and the 18-karat gold proof mark, were some tiny marks scratched in the polished gold with a sharp instrument. Examined with a jeweler's loupe they proved to be two Ss or more likely two crude lightning flashes, followed by a number: clearly the watch had been taken, like all valuables, from a man entering a concentration camp, and was found valuable enough by a prisoner-jeweler to receive an SS store number before being sent back to Germany for resale. Was the owner Jewish? Very likely. Was the jeweler who appraised the watch in the camp a Jew, too? Almost certainly. Most of the jewelers and watchmakers of prewar Poland were. I was holding in my hand a piece of European history. It would have been interesting to learn the identity of the man whose initials were engraved on the watch and how it made its way from a German concentration camp in Poland to New York, but some things are undiscoverable. Still, though objects are supposed to be neutral, I could never pick it up or wear it without a certain frisson or without in some way thinking about the Holocaust and of the forces that brought an upper-middle-class Polish Jew, probably a professional of some kind (it was not a cheap watch), to one of the SS death camps, where he lost both his watch and his life. Watches very often have lots to say about the people who owned them once we decipher their marks and engravings, which is one of their fascinations.

And, in general, watches survive vastly better than do the people who owned them or for whom they were made. I have seen come up for auction both the watch that Breguet made for poor Marie Antoinette and a watch that a Breguet rival made for her husband Louis XVI—the latter, because of its complexity, not completed until several years after the king's execution on what is now la place de la Concorde (Marie Antoinette's followed not long afterward). Watches of the Russian royal family surface for sale from time to time, though the owners were murdered at Ekaterinburg. Though Hitler apparently did not wear a watch himself, at least so far as one is able to observe from photographs, elaborately inscribed watches presented *by* him come up for sale rather often, some genuine, some not. The heavy gold hunter of King Alexander I of Serbia survives in perfect condition, with two enamel portraits, on one side of his young wife Draga—the watch was a gift from her to him—looking slightly plump, but very beautiful, with a tiara on her head and a diamond choker around her neck, and on the other side of the young king himself, looking, with his weak chin, full moustache, and pince-nez, like an irritable schoolmaster, despite all his decorations and orders. The watch survives intact, although the royal couple was brutally defenestrated from their palace in Belgrade—the king held on with his fingers to the window ledge until one of the conspirators in the palace coup d'état, which brought to the throne the even more ill-fated Karageorgevich dynasty, finally chopped them off with his saber, dropping him to the pavement. The king and queen did not survive the fall, but the watch did. Watches—and this is part of their fascination—last a good deal longer than people unless they are subsumed in fires or go down with their owners on the *Titanic*.

Owning a watch collection is therefore an effort at *preserving* something for a limited period of time. The fact that very few watch collections survive more than one generation is borne out by the auction catalogs themselves, in which almost everything of any value or interest is being sold by the estate, the widow, or the children of a collector. In a sense, all good watches go back into the pool again, to be plucked out by some new connoisseur who is building a collection of his own, a *cycle* in which a certain number (very large, admittedly) of valuable objects vanish for a time, only to reappear for sale five, ten, or twenty years later. Even the watches of such prodigious watch collectors as Packard and Graves come up for sale eventually, including Henry Graves's famous $11 million plus Patek pocket watch with twenty-four complications. One might have thought that a man who devoted so much of his life to building up his collection as Graves did would have found some way of preserving the collection—the Graves Museum of Time?—but it seldom happens, and if Graves, of all people, didn't manage to do it, the rest of us are unlikely to. (Graves, apparently, had second thoughts about the famous watch with twenty-four complications, and was tempted to throw it into a lake after the Lindbergh kidnapping made him fear it would attract attention to his two daughters.)

Given this, the first rule of collecting ought to be, like that of the physician, do no harm. Watches ought not to be modified, overcleaned, overrestored, or misused. If they are worth collecting in the first place, they should be looked after without being "restored" to the point where they no longer resemble what they originally were. Cases shouldn't be polished until they look like mirrors; dials shouldn't be altered or "refinished" so they look like new; inscriptions and monograms shouldn't be filled in or polished off—the goal is to pass the object on in good condition, in *better* condition if possible, but not totally changed like a woman who has undergone an over-ambitious face lift.

A friend of mine has a couple of dozen wristwatches, from which he carefully selects a different one every day depending on his mood and on what he's wearing. He knows perfectly well that most people won't notice, but he doesn't care. He's doing it for *his* satisfaction.

I am the same way. My collection of pocket watches, which is of modest size, nevertheless presents me with a certain amount of choice. For example, because I don't wear a waistcoat in the summer, I tend to wear a smaller watch, and usually carry it in my righthand trouser pocket, with a chain linked to a belt loop. The bigger watches make a bulge in the pocket, so I usually pick a simple minute repeater or, better yet, my two-train minute repeater or the Vanderbilt split-second minute-repeater chronograph, which is unusually small for such a complex watch. In the colder months, I wear a waistcoat, specially made with a lined pocket for a watch and an extra buttonhole for the chain to pass through, which is good looking and practical, and was the way waistcoats were made until after World War I. This allows me to wear the bigger watches with comfort and without any discernable bulge—a minute-repeater hunter, for example, or a doctor's hunter with the dial marked off for measuring the patient's pulse. The Vanderbilt watch came with its own Tiffany pink gold chain, so it serves double use as an evening dress watch, with the chain looped across the front of a black silk evening waistcoat.

The selection of the right watch to wear is a pleasant early-morning puzzle, one of the things that makes a watch collection rewarding. Should I take *this* one or take *that* one? Rose gold or yellow gold? And for the collector of pocket watches, there's the additional pleasure of an accompanying collection of watch chains—Leontine chains, Guard chains, or Prince Albert chains, which have heavy gold links, usually becoming smaller and smaller toward the center of the chain, and some kind of sliding bar to put through the waistcoat buttonhole so that the chain hangs across the waistcoat in two equal arcs. I count no fewer than fifty-three separate kinds and patterns of watch chain in the catalogue of E. W. Streeter, Jeweler, of 18 New Bond Street, London, dated 1885, not to speak of twenty different grades of men's English-made pocket watches, each one available in open face, demihunter, or hunter case, with an infinite variety of engraving patterns, plus monogramming and coats of arms.

Chains were such a normal accoutrement to men's wear up to World War I that there are many still around—at any watch or jewelry show, you will see dozens or even hundreds of them—and they're not really much more expensive to buy than the value of the gold, so the collector of pocket watches will have no difficulty in assembling an interesting collection of chains.

Equally important—but not easy to find—are the suede-lined Morocco leather open-topped pouches into which the Georgians, Victorians, and Edwardians slipped their watches to protect them from being scratched by the chains, loose change, or keys. These pouches come in a variety of colors, often with handsome stamped gold initials, and, of course, they must fit the watch in question, so don't buy one without trying your watch in it. A certain number of leather craftsman who make boxes for the jewelry trade also make pocket watch pouches, and it's well worth having one to fit each pocket watch in your collection.

Those who collect wristwatches and wear them are often equally fussy about leather watch straps. After all, if you've bought a wristwatch for six figures, you don't want to put a cheap, mass-produced strap on it, do you? The best thing from the point of view of authenticity is to go back to the manufacturer, but there also exist, particularly in Italy, a few houses that specialize in custom-made watch straps in exotic leathers, hand sewn and lined, and perfectly fitted to the watch. (Just don't ever forget that the little buckle that goes on the strap is supposed to match the watch and must be stamped with the watch manufacturer's name, so if you have a platinum Lange watch, don't ever let the little buckle out of your hands when you're having your watch strap changed. Collectors care about this kind of detail, and those little buckles can cost hundreds of dollars to replace—when they *can* be replaced; for old watches, they very often can't.)

It makes good sense to keep a polishing cloth handy to wipe your fingerprints and any trace of dirt or perspiration off the watch before you put it away at the end of the day. Most jewelry stores carry pretty good cloths for buffing gold jewelry, which do the job very well, though the preferred brand is Selvyt, an English polishing cloth that can be found in most good jewelry stores or the silver counter of department stores. Resist the temptation to give the watch a good hard polish every time you put it away, particularly with the kinds of polishing cloth that contain jeweler's rouge (Selvyt doesn't). Just wipe it and wrap it in a cloth or a jewelry pouch. The big ornamental leather cases for keeping watches seem to me like an invitation to thieves. A locked drawer and a good alarm system are the best bet. That and having them insured at full value, of course.

Perhaps the best and most basic thing is to keep a file on each watch—bill of sale, insurance appraisal, all the correspondence and historical research relating to the watch, and a color photocopy of the watch, front and back. Elementary as this paperwork may seem, it will pay dividends in case of theft, and I'm astonished that so many people neglect to do it.

Having done all that, enjoy your ownership and wear what you own!

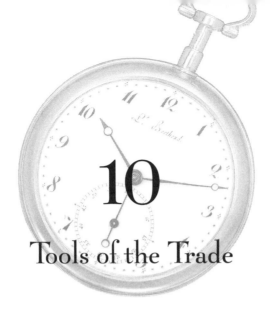

10

Tools of the Trade

*U*NLIKE MOST hobbies, collecting watches doesn't require a huge amount of equipment. As I've already mentioned, the right kind of polishing cloth *is* important (following the sound principle of "less is more," it should be old, frequently washed, and contain no abrasives), but equally important and useful is a soft pad, rather like the ones that camera stores used to have on the counter, though a well-washed old face towel will serve just as well. This pad merely assures that you don't scratch the watch when you put it down on your desk to examine it or clean it and that there is something soft beneath it just in case it slips out of your fingers (which has been known to happen, alas).

Tools should be restricted very severely to a jeweler's pocketknife, with a specially shaped blade for prying open tight covers on pocket watches and older wristwatches. Even that makes me nervous, though. First of all, there's an art to doing it, rather like shucking an oyster, and, second, more watches are ruined by bungling, careless attempts to pry the back open than by any other cause. A deep gouge in the metal is almost impossible to repair or polish out. Still, on occasion, it's necessary to open up a watch and look at its serial number or at any special inscription on the inner side of the back cover or the movement. The essential trick is to wrap the blade of the knife in a thickness of plastic—a small Ziploc bag is perfect—then gently but firmly push the edge into the right spot until the watch pops open. Have somebody who knows show you how before trying! It's not a question of physical force—it's a trick, which you either learn or not. If you can't do it within the first few minutes, give it up and take it to a watchmaker. Some people can do this with a thumbnail, but I can't—my thumbnails aren't strong enough. The main thing is not to engage in a trial of strength with the watch—opening it shouldn't require brute force applied with the edge of a knife blade, which is almost surely going to lead to trouble. If you're going to practice, practice on cheap watch cases, not the $11 million Patek you've just bought.

The special knife is really the only tool you ought to need. Unless you've had a long apprenticeship in Switzerland as a watchmaker, do not even *dream* of touching the movement of the watch. Obeying that simple injunction will not only safeguard your collection, but make it unnecessary to purchase a kit of tiny watchmaker's screwdrivers, pliers, and such like. In fact, it's far better not to own any of these things, which puts temptation out of reach. Watch repair *can* be learned, of course—both King George III of Great Britain and Louis XVI of France took it up in middle age—but, as you will recall, George III went mad and lost his North American colonies, and Louis XVI was guillotined, so it may be that learning how to repair watches takes up too much time to leave any over for your normal business affairs. Certainly, that appears to have been the case with those two unhappy kings. I think the best thing is to develop a good relationship with a watchmaker who is skilled at working with vintage watches and has the time and patience to get them running correctly. Not many such watchmakers are around, even in big cities, but a good local jeweler may have the names of one or two of them.

In any event, the three basics of watch ownership are: (1) do nothing that requires force; (2) keep your fingers off the movement; and (3) don't drop the watch.

When winding a watch, for example, do it slowly and gently and stop at the first sign of resistance—most watches have at some point or another been damaged by overwinding or by winding with too much force. From this caveat derives a fourth sensible rule: do not do anything to a watch if you are in a hurry, in a temper, or in a distracted frame of mind. Watches require complete concentration and gentle handling, always, even if you're doing something as simple as winding them up or resetting the time.

It will pay dividends to ensure, even for basic tasks, that you have (1) enough light, (2) a clear, uncluttered desk space, suitably cushioned in case the watch slips out of your fingers, (3) time, and (4) a firm degree of concentration. Do *not,* for example, try to wind your watch while speaking on the telephone or reset it while reading your mail—the consequences of divided attention are almost always a trip to the watch repairman and a big bill. With older watches, bear in mind that all repairs are complicated by age and the lack of replacement parts, which will result in the watch being out of your hands for a long time.

For those who own watches with tiny dimples placed in the edge of the case to reset the date, the day of the week, or the phases of the moon, strong wooden toothpicks will do very nicely and have the great advantage that they can't scratch the case if they slip in your fingers, unlike the metal picks often provided with the watch. A box of toothpicks, kept handy, will save a lot of trouble and grief.

A good strong desk light is, of course, indispensable, preferably one with a magnifying glass that can be swung into position. Any hobbyist store will likely carry several models. In addition, a good jeweler's loupe is an essential tool to have on hand, both for examining watches and for trying to decipher tiny inscriptions and numbers that may be almost unreadable with the naked eye (and are likely to become even less readable as the naked eye ages). Certainly you shouldn't buy an expensive vintage watch without examining it carefully for scratches, cracks in the dial, damaged hands, or obvious repairs, or before having at least a cursory look at the movement to see if the slots in the screw heads are clean and if any rust is present. More than this can and should be left to a skilled appraiser or a watchmaker, but a good loupe at least lets you see any signs of damage, bad handling, or careless repair, as well as occasionally revealing important information that everybody else may have ignored.

I personally find that a reliable time source is a handy thing to have at hand—in my case a modern quartz naval chronometer—so that I have a single time against which to measure all my watches. It isn't so much a question of accuracy, as of *consistency.*

I think it probably helps, by the way, not to obsess about accuracy. Watches vary in their timekeeping because of the position they're kept in or the weather or the temperature or the residual level of magnetism, and even the best wristwatches are influenced by the amount of physical activity you do while wearing them and perhaps by other influences of the body conveyed to a delicate mechanism strapped directly to the skin. A good watch will keep time very well under any and all conditions, but checking it constantly against a known time source and worrying about a fraction of a second difference is basically a recipe for driving yourself crazy. If we're expected for lunch at 12:30, we should be able to rely on our watch, but most of us don't need and wouldn't recognize accuracy to a thousandth of a second, or even a hundredth of a second. I know a great many people whose pleasure in their expensive watches is spoiled by expecting a wristwatch to keep time like the U.S. government's atomic clock, despite the fact that they're going from a warm office to the cold street all day long or wearing the watch in the shower or banging against things when they exercise or standing half a dozen times a day next to a magnetic source, from a copying machine to a kitchen magnet. A good watch is capable of dealing with all these things, but not without minute variations. What matters most is its consistency—its ability, in short, to measure one exact minute or one exact second without any significant variation. No mechanical watch placed on a human being's wrist can ever equal in accurate timekeeping a clock that is fixed in place and not exposed to the elements. Pocket watches do slightly better, as a rule, precisely because they're fixed in one position, upright, in a waistcoat pocket and also protected from temperature changes by your body heat— also, being larger, they're easier for a watchmaker to adjust. All the same, if what you want is accuracy to the thousandth of a second, what you need is one of those electronic wristwatches that displays digital time controlled by receiving a continuous signal from the U.S. government's atomic clock—but when was the last time you really needed to know the time to a thousandth of a second, after all? Like most interesting artifacts, watches are a compromise, not a complete solution. Just as there is no way to combine the load-carrying benefits of a bus with the handling and speed of a sports car, there is no way to combine small size, dazzling elegance, reliability of timekeeping despite movement and exposure to the elements, and 100 percent perfect accuracy all in one package on the wrist or even in the waistcoat pocket.

If you're going to collect watches at all seriously, you need to build up a suitable reference library, both on the general subject of watches and on the specific makes of watches you're collecting. These books are not necessarily easy to find, but a very reliable source is Mr. Tran Duy Ly, Arlington Books, Tennessee. His Web site is arlingtonbooks.com. His daughter Bettina Ly also has a book company devoted to watches in Tennessee, called US Books, and can be reached at usbooks.com.

Books absolutely necessary to the collector include the latest edition of *Britten's Old Clocks and Watches and Their Makers* (Ninth edition, Bloomsbury, 1986); *Technique and*

History of the Swiss Watch (Spring Books, Hamlyn, 1970); and
Time in Gold—Wristwatches (Schiffer, 1990).

TRULY, WATCHES are wonderful objects, and no auction catalog ever fails to produce at least a couple of them that would be wonderful to own. As I write, I am looking at the latest Phillips auction catalog (itself something of a work of art), which includes not only the Rolex of the late Emperor Bao Dai of Vietnam—an extraordinary yellow gold Oyster perpetual calendar wristwatch with moon phases, with a black dial set with diamond indexes—but also a 1952 "first series" rose gold Patek Philippe perpetual calendar chronograph wristwatch, valued at more than $1.3 million (of the 349 watches of this "reference," or model, the celebrated number 2499, the "first series" constituted less than 10 percent of that total, of which only 3 were made in rose gold, hence the rarity factor), and also a truly wonderful Breguet pocket watch manufactured in 1804 and sold to James Watt, the inventor of the steam engine, on his trip to Paris on 14 Floréal, Year 12 (France was still on the revolutionary calendar). Watt's watch has none of Breguet's famous complications; it's relatively plain and simple (insofar as anything made by Breguet is simple), but exquisitely made and finished, a work of art as much as a watch. As for its mechanical perfection, it seems unlikely that Watt—who in 1804 was already world famous for his invention—would have gone to Breguet unless he was convinced that Breguet's watches were the finest and the most advanced in the world—as indeed they were at the time.

It's hard to imagine a collector whose attention wouldn't be drawn to at least one of these watches, two of which (the Bao Dai Rolex and the Watt Breguet) have, quite apart from their own special qualities, substantial historical interest, and one of which represents the rarest of the rare in modern wristwatches. Although the Patek wristwatch is worth nearly ten times what the Rolex is worth, the Rolex is an even more remarkable rarity. Rolex made only three watches of this type; in two of them, the diamond markers on the dial are on the odd numerals, but on this watch they are, for some reason, on the even numbers, which means that because there is a diamond set at "twelve," the Rolex crown and name had to be moved down, and the words "Superlative chronometer officially certified" were moved onto the small dial on the bottom, below the window for the moon phases. It is, therefore, in every possible way, a unique watch, never duplicated by Rolex.

Incidentally, the same catalog also contains five silver pocket watches made from scratch by students at the Swiss Watchmaking School in Le Locle, all of them of exquisite hand workmanship and containing a variety of unusual and interesting complications, and all valued at between $700 and $2,000, so you wouldn't have to spend in the six figures (or the seven figures as for the Patek) to come home with something unusual, unique, and very special from this auction, in addition to having a watch that you can wear and use for the rest of your life, that nobody else is going to own one like, that is only likely to go up and up in value over the years, and that will give you satisfaction, faithful service, and accurate timekeeping.

If I weren't already committed to Patek pocket watches from the "grand period," I would take a close look at the watches made by the students at Le Locle, not just because they're beautiful and genuinely handmade, but because the

A silver chronograph watch with counter, made by a pupil in the watchmaking school at Le Locle in Switzerland, ca. 1915. Note the superb craftsmanship and elegance, for a relatively modest price.
(Courtesy of Phillips, de Pury & Luxembourg)

students and teachers at watchmaking schools in Switzerland and Germany have been making unique watches like this for a couple of hundred years—it's the watchmaking equivalent of a Ph.D. thesis—so a collection of them would be a wonderful thing....And the prices for most of them are still relatively modest....

But hold me back! I already *have* a collection. I don't need another.

Still, for somebody else—*you*, perhaps—it might be just the right starting point, who knows?

MEASURING TIME is perhaps the best way we have of understanding it. We cannot grasp it or change it or slow it down; it does indeed, in the words of the hymn, "bear all its sons away," and daughters, too, but the effort to measure it exactly has given birth to many of the most extraordinary and elaborate of human inventions and to a world in which beauty and precision are uniquely combined. In the sense that these are major themes of life, no watch, however mass-produced, is ever boring—each one represents yet another attempt to answer an ancient need to define what is invisible and can be understood only mathematically: the measurement of time.

In collecting watches, we are paying homage to human genius and skill, and to the fleeting quality of life. Few kinds of collecting offer such a deep philosophical pleasure.

A Useful Glossary
of Watch Terms*

ADJUSTED: Term applied to watch movements and some small clock movements to indicate that they have been corrected for various errors, such as isochronism, temperature, and positions.

AGATE: A stone which is a variety of chalcedony, usually containing a pattern such as banding, eyes, etc.

ALARM: An attachment to a watch whereby, at a predetermined time, a bell is sounded.

ALLOY: The mixing of more than one metal in order to produce one of greater hardness, malleability, and/or durability.

ANIMATED: Imitating or giving life-like movement to a watch dial. (Usually Comic Character).

ANTI-MAGNETIC: A balance and spring composed of alloys that will not retain magnetism after being put through a magnetic field.

* *Reprinted from* Patek Philippe—Identification and Price Guide, *by Roy Ehrhardt and Joe DeMesy, copyright MCMXCI by Roy Ehrhardt, by permission of Heart of America Press, Roy Ehrhardt*

APPLIED FIGURES: Figures which have been attached to the dial, usually with screws or small bolts with nuts.

ARABIC FIGURES: Figures on a dial, such as a 1, 2, 3, as opposed to Roman Numerals, such as I, II, V, IX.

ART DECO: A style of design between 1910–1935, most importantly influenced by cubist geometry.

AUTOMATIC WINDING: See Self-winding.

BAGUETTE: A step cut used for rectangular stones, of a small size.

BALANCE: The oscillating wheel of a watch, which in conjunction with the hairspring (balance spring) regulates the speed of a clock or watch. May be made bimetallic to compensate for temperate changes and may be studded with screws for regulation.

BEARING: The support for a pivot or arbor. Jewelled bearings are used where there is danger of rapid wear on the pivots of fast moving parts such as the balance staff and also train wheel pivots.

BEAT: The sound of the ticking of a watch, caused by the teeth of the escape wheel striking the pallets or arms of the escapement.

BEVELLED: Inclining from a right line to form a slant.

BEZEL: The groove in which the glass (crystal) of a watch is set.

BREGUET: A horological genius of the late 18th and early 19th century. The name applied to the type of hairspring which has its last outer coil raised above the body of the spring and curved inwards.

BRIDGE: Upper plated in a $\frac{3}{4}$ plate watch for the support of the wheels, or pallet. Always has at least two feet or supports.

BRILLIANT CUT: The most beautiful form of cutting a diamond. It is also used for other clear stones. The standard brilliant has 58 facets, 33 in the crown and 25 in the base.

BUBBLEBACK: Slang term for the early Rolex Oyster Perpetual (ca. 1930 to 1950's).

CALENDAR, MOONPHASE: A disk, usually with a blue background, containing the moon phases and further decoration of stars which rotates one complete turn per month. Located at the 6th or 12th hour position. In reality, the moon rotates around the earth in 29 days, 12 hours, 44 minutes and $2\frac{4}{5}$ seconds.

CALENDAR, PERPETUAL: A perpetual calendar mechanism is self-adjusting, that is to say it automatically indicates the months of varying length and is self-correcting for leap years.

CALENDAR, PERPETUAL RETROGRADE: The date hand moves through an arc on the dial and returns to 1 after reaching the proper date 28, 29, 39, or 31.

CALENDAR, SIMPLE: Automatically registers one or all of the following: day, date, month, and moonphase, and must be manually adjusted for months having total days other than 31.

CALIBER: The size or factory number of a watch movement.

CAP JEWEL: The flat solid jewel upon which rests the pivot end. Also call the "Endstone".

CENTER-SECONDS HAND: Sometimes called sweep-seconds hand. Mounted on the center post of watches.

CHAMPFERRED: A bevelled or sloped edge.

CHAMPLEVE: Enameling done by cutting grooves in the metal into which the ground enamel is melted. The surface is then ground and polished.

CHAPTER RING: The circle on the dial that contains the numbers for the hours and minutes. So called because in early clocks it was a separate ring attached to the dial.

CHROMIUM: Very hard crystalline metallic chemical element with a high resistance to corrosion, uses as plating on wristwatch cases.

CHRONOGRAPH: A mechanical watch with hour and minute hand and center sweep-second hand which can be controlled by one or more special buttons, in the side of the case or through the crown. The sweep-second hand may be started, stopped, and made to return to zero without interfering with the timekeeping of the watch.

CHRONOGRAPH, SIMPLIFIED (One Button): Sweep-second hand runs continuously on this single button chronograph when at rest. Press completely down to return to zero, hold down until timing begins upon release, push down halfway to stop, release to start again, or all the way down to flyback. Usually of cheaper construction.

CHRONOGRAPH, SPLIT-SECOND: Same as chronograph but is fitted with an additional center sweep-second hand (total of 2) with separate controls (buttons) to permit the timing of two events simultaneously. Example: The split-second chronograph with two chronograph hands permits ascertaining, in races of all kinds, the times of arrival of competitors following closely upon each other's heels. The chronograph is set in motion by pressing a button whereupon both hands begin to move. At the arrival of the first competitor the one hand is stopped by pressing this button again and the time is read off. When the button is pressed a third time this hand catches up with the other in one jump, after which both move on together. At the arrival of the second competitor the first hand is again stopped and the time noted down. In this way, any desired number of time recordings can be made. A button fitted in the winder serves to return both hands to zero.

CLICK: A spring tensioned pawl holding the ratchet wheel against the tension of the main-spring, enabling the spring to be wound, usually making the clicking noise as the watch is wound.

CLOISONNE ENAMEL: A type of enamel work in which thin strips of metal are soldered to the base to form the outlines of the design. Colored enamel is then placed in each section.

COCK: An overhanging support for a bearing such as the balance cock; a cock has a support at one end only.

COMPENSATING BALANCE: A balance with a bimetallic rim made of brass and steel. The diameter increases or decreases with changes in temperature to compensate for these changes.

CONICAL PIVOT: A pivot which curves back into the main body of its arbor, such as those used with cap jewels. (Balance staff pivots).

CONVERTIBLE CASE: Watch case built into a sliding frame allowing the dial side to be turned over facing the wrist to protect it.

CONVEX: A domed surface.

CROWN: A grooved circular piece fastened to the stem for winding the watch. (Slang term "Winding Knob or Button").

CURB PINS: The two regulator pins almost pinching the hairspring.

CURVEX: Case with a slightly curved back to fit the wrist better. (Patented by Gruen)

CUSHION: Square form with rounded edges.

DETENT: The setting lever. A detainer or pawl.

DIAL TRAIN: The train of wheels under the dial which moves the hands. The cannon pinion hour wheels, minute wheel and pinion.

DIAMOND DIAL: Dial set with diamonds for markers, numerals, etc.

DIGITAL: See Jump Hour.

DOCTOR'S WATCH: See Duo-Dial.

DOLLAR WATCH: A practical timepiece with a non-jewelled movement. The case and movement an integral unit with a dial of paper on brass or other inexpensive material. Ingersoll sold his first Dollar watch for $1 in 1892. (Taken from "The Watch That Made the Dollar Famous" by George E. Townsend).

DOUBLE-ROLLER ESCAPEMENT: A form of lever escapement in which a separate roller is used for the safety action.

DUO-DIAL: Separate hour and seconds dials. (Slang term "Doctor's Watch").

DUPLEX ESCAPEMENT: A watch escapement in which the escape wheel has two sets of teeth. One set locks the wheel by pressing on the balance staff. The other set gives impulse to the balance. The balance receives impulse at every other vibration.

EBAUCHE: A term used by Swiss watch manufacturers to denote the raw movement without jewels, escapement, plating, and engraving. The manufacturers supply their ebauches to trade name importers in the U.S.A., and other countries who have them finishes, jewelled, dialed, cased, etc., and engraved with their own (advertised) name brands.

ELINVAR: A non rusting, non-magnetizing alloy containing iron, nickel, chromium, tungsten, silicon, and carbon. Used for balance and balance spring. (Hamilton)

ELONGATED: The state of being stretched out or lengthened.

EMBOSSED: To carve, raise or print so that it is raised above the surface.

EMERALD CUT: A style of rectangular or square cut, featuring steps of elongated facets.

ENAMEL: (Soft) A soluble paint used in dials. (Hard) A porcelain-like paint used as an ornamental coating, acid-resisting and durable.

ENGINE-TURNED: A form of machine engraving similar to etching.

ENGRAVED: To cut into, to form a pattern or design either by hand or machine.

FILIGREE: Ornamental open work executed in fine gold or silver wire.

FLAT HAIRSPRING: A hairspring whose spirals develop on a flat surface. As opposed to the overcoil (Breguet) hairspring.

FOURTH WHEEL: Usually the wheel which carries the second hand and drives the escape wheel; it is the fourth wheel from the great wheel in the going train of a watch.

GERMAN SILVER: A silver-white alloy composed mainly of copper, zinc, and nickel, called silver but containing none.

GILDED: To give a golden hue: gold plating.

GILDING: The process of coating the surface of metal with gold by painting on a mixture of mercury and gold and then heating to evaporate the mercury.

GOLD: Pure 24K gold is yellow in color. It is very soft and not acceptable for use in articles subject to wear, unless alloyed with harder metal. The choice of alloy metals determines the color of the gold.

GOLD-FILLED: Another name for rolled gold.

GOLD PLATED: Electro-plated a few thousandths of an inch thick with pure or alloyed gold.

GRANDE SONNIERIE: A quarter hour repeater: a type of striking in which the first hour struck is repeated at each quarter. Present day usage sometimes applies the term to a quarter hour which can be made to strike at will.

GREEN GOLD (GG): True green gold cannot be made of less fineness than 17 karat; usually made of 10 to 14 karat gold, alloyed with silver to make it as pale as possible and then the finished piece is electroplated with 18 karat green gold. True green gold is 17 parts pure gold and 7 parts pure silver.

GREENWICH CIVIL TIME: Also called Universal Time (UT). It is Local mean time as measured at Grenwich, England. (G.C.T.)

HAIRSPRING: The spiraled spring attached to the balance to govern the speed of the balance oscillations.

HEXAGONAL: Six sided.

HOUR RECORDER: Small offset hour recorder dial has an indicator hand that advances one hour marker each time the minute recorder counts off 60 minutes. Usually placed over the 6th hour marker.

HUNTING CASE: Spring-loaded lid or cover over the face of the watch.

INDEPENDENT SECONDS-BEATING: Fitted with a special center sweep seconds hand that advances by one jump every second. Sometimes called "Jump Second".

INDEX: The regulator scale. Used to help in adjusting the regulation. Most balance wheel clocks and watches had indexes.

INTEGRAL: A part that is permanently attached to another part, thus becoming one. As in a bracelet permanently attached to the head of a wristwatch.

INVAR: A steel alloy containing about 36 percent nickel that remains the same length at different temperatures. Used in the making of balance wheels. Also used for pendulum rods in clocks for temperature compensation. Similar to Elinvar.

ISOCHRONISM: Quality of keeping equal time during the normal run of the mainspring, usually the qualities of a well-formed overcoil hairspring.

JEWEL: Synthetic or semi-precious stones used for bearings in watches and precision clocks.

JUMP HOUR (OR DIGITAL): The hour indicator advances instantaneously at the beginning of the hour.

JUMP SECOND: See Independent Seconds-Beating.

LAPIS LAZULI: Synonym for lazurite, or ultra marine. An azure-blue stone with vitreous lustre, sometimes with gold specks used in jewelry and an occasional wristwatch dial.

LIGNE ('''): A Swiss watch size, 2.2558mm, or 0.0888in.

LUMINOUS: Giving off light; glows in the dark. (See Radium).

MAINSPRING: The flat, ribbon-like tempered steel spring wound inside the barrel and used to drive the train wheels. Most American clocks eliminated the barrel.

MARQUISE CUT: A cut for diamonds in which the stone is brilliantly faceted and then shaped like an elongated almond or tear-drop with pointed ends.

MATTE: A dull or flat finish.

MEAN TIME: When all days and hours are of equal length. This is opposed to Solar Time where all days are not of equal length.

MEANTIME SCREWS: The adjustable screws in a better grade balance used to bring the watch to close time without the use of the regulator. Sometimes called "timing screws".

MIDDLE-TEMPERATURE ERROR: The temperature error between the extremes of heat and cold characteristic of a compensating balance and steel balance spring.

MILLED: Having the edge transversely grooved.

MINUTE RECORDING: Small offset minute recorder dial that advances 1 minute with each revolution made by the second hand. Usually one of three types: 1) Continuous; 2) Semi-instantaneous; 3) Instantaneous. Usually placed by the third-hour marker.

NICKEL SILVER: An alloy of nickel, copper, and zinc; usually 65 percent copper, 5–25 percent nickel, and 10–30 percent zinc, containing no silver.

NON-MAGNETIC: See Antimagnetic.

OCTAGONAL: Eight sided.

OPEN FACE: A watch dial with the figure "12" at the winding stem.

OVAL: Elongated circle.

PALLADIUM: One of the platinum group of metals and much lighter. Will not tarnish and can be deposited on other metal by electroplating. Value is less than gold or platinum.

PAVE: A style of setting stones where a number of small stones are set as close together as possible; to completely cover.

PENNYWEIGHT (DWT): A unit in troy weight equal to twenty-four grains or one-twentieth of an ounce.

PERPETUAL WINDING: See Self-winding.

PHILLIPS' SPRING: A balance spring with terminal curves formed on lines laid down by M. Phillips. The term "Phillips' curve" is rarely used.

PIN PALLET: The lever escapement wherein the pallet has upright pins instead of horizontally set jewels. Used in alarm clocks and non-jeweled watches.

PINK GOLD (PG): (See Rose Gold).

POISING: An operation to adjust the balance so that all weights are counterpoised. In other words, statically balancing a wheel or balance in a watch.

POSITION TIMING: Adjusting a watch so that it keeps precise time when the watch is placed in a given position. Adjusted to three, four, five, or six positions.

POWER RESERVE INDICATOR: See Up & Down Indicator.

PURSE WATCH: Folding, covered, or otherwise protected watch for carrying in the purse or pocket. (Example: Movado Ermeto).

QUICK TRAIN: A watch movement beating five times per second, or 18,000 per hour.

RADIUM: A radioactive metallic element that gives off light. Used on luminous dials.

REGULATOR: Part of the balance bridge which resembles a racquette (racket) and contains vertical pins which straddle the hairspring. When the regulator moves towards the stud, the effective length of the hairspring is made longer and the balance slows in speed; when the pins are moved farther from the stud, the hairspring is made shorter and the watch goes faster.

REPEATING WATCHES: Usually one of six types: 1) Quarter repeater—striking a deep note for the last hour (as shown on the dial) and two shrill notes, ting-tang for each quarter; 2) Half-Quarter Repeater—striking the last hour, the quarters, and a single blow for the nearest half-quarter; 3) Five-Minute Repeaters—striking a deep note for the last hour (as shown on the dial) and one shrill note for each five minutes after the hour; 4) Minute Repeater—striking a deep note for the last hour (as shown on the dial), two shrill notes for each minute past the last quarter. The most complicated and popular today; 5) Clock Watches—the hours and quarters are struck automatically as the watch goes but the hours, quarters, and minutes can be repeated at will by a slide in the case band; 6) Carillon—the quarters are struck on two, three, or four different notes. Sometimes known as "Cathedrals."

REPOUSSE: Decorating metal by hammering out a design behind or on the reverse side in order to create a design in relief.

REVERSO: See Convertible Case.

ROLLED GOLD: A metal plate formed by bonding a thin sheet of gold to one or both sides of a backing metal. Made by rolling the sandwich until the gold is at the desired thinness.

ROSE CUT: Method of faceting stones with many small and usually not precision cuts.

ROSE GOLD: Karat gold alloyed with copper.

SAPPHIRE CRYSTAL (SYNTHETIC SAPPHIRE CRYSTAL): Extremely hard material used for watch crystals.

SELF-WINDING: Wristwatch that will wind itself by use of a rotor or other mechanical means by swinging movement of the arm. If worn by a normally active person for four hours, it will remain running for 30 hours.

SETTING LEVER: The detent which fits into the slot of the stem and pushes down the clutch lever.

SILVERED: Silver in color, not necessarily in metal content.

SIZES OF WATCHES: The American sizes are based on 30ths of an inch. The Europeans use the ligne which is equal to .089 inches or 2.255 millimeters. In every case, the diameter is measured across the outside or largest part of the lower plate of the watch, right under the dial. In oval or other odd shaped movements, the size is measured across the smaller axis.

STAFF: A pivoted arbor or axle usually referred to the axle of the balance: as the "balance staff."

STERLING: The minimum standard of purity of fineness of English silver; 925 parts pure silver to 1000 parts.

STOPWATCH: A simple form of chronograph with controlled starting and stopping of the hands; sometimes also stopping the balance wheel. A timer in pocket watch form.

STOPWORK: The mechanism on a barrel of a watch that permits only the central portion of the mainspring to be wound, thus utilizing that portion of the spring whose power is less erratic.

SUBSIDIARY SECONDS: Small dial, usually opposite the winding crown on a chronograph and at the 6th hour position on a time only watch, that indicates the seconds and makes one revolution per minute.

SUNK SECONDS: The small second dial which is depressed to avoid the second hand from interfering with the progress of the hour and minute hand.

SWEEP SECONDS: See Center Seconds.

TANK CASE: Flat, square, conservatively tailored case. (Introduced by Cartier, Patented by Gruen).

TIGER EYE: Silicified fibrous variety of "Riebeckite". A stone that when cut properly displays an eye-like effect.

TIMEPIECE: Any watch that does not strike or chime.

TIMING SCREWS: Screws used to bring a watch to time, sometimes called the mean-time screws.

TONNEAU: Shape of case with its widest point across the center and tapering towards square ends.

TOURBILLON: A watch in which the escapement, mounted on a cage attached to the fourth pinion, revolves around the mounted and stationary fourth wheel.

TRAIN: A combination of two or more wheels and pinions, geared together and transmitting power from one part of a mechanism to another, usually from the power source (weight or spring) to the escapement.

TROY WEIGHT: The system of weights commonly used in England and the United States for gold and silver. One pound equals 12 ounces, 1 ounce equals 20 pennyweights (dwt.) and 1 pennyweight equals 24 grains (gr.).

TU-TONE: Two colors of metal in the case or dial finish.

UP AND DOWN INDICATOR: The semi-circular indicator hand or window indicator that tells how much the mainspring has been unwound and thus indicates when the spring should be wound. On wristwatches usually indicates how many hours are left. (Same as Power-Reserve Indicator).

VERMEIL: Gilded silver.

VIBRATING TOOL: A master balance of certified accuracy as to vibrations per hour which is mounted in a box with glass top. The box may be swiveled to set the balance into its vibratory arcs. The balance to be compared or vibrated is suspended by its hairspring attached to a scaffold and when the box is twisted on its platform both balance may be compared (in speed) with the master balance and its hairspring lengthened or shortened until both balances swing in unison.

WATERPROOF: Airtight so that no water can enter.

WHITE GOLD (WG): 24 karat yellow gold alloyed with nickel to make 14 or 18 karat white gold.

Index

Index